Palestinian Refugees and Peace Process

A FINAL STATUS ISSUES PAPER

Palestinian Refugees and the Peace Process

Elia Zureik

Institute for Palestine Studies
Washington, D.C.

ISBN: 0-88728-266-0

Printed in the United States of America

Contents

Publisher's Note

This paper was prepared as part of the Institute for Palestine Studies (IPS) Final Status Issues project. The project combines research, documentation, and policy seminars with the aim of raising awareness of and contributing to the peace process on key final status issues. The IPS thanks the Diana Tamari-Sabbagh Foundation and the Ford Foundation for their assistance.

Elia Zureik is professor of sociology at Queens University in Kingston, Ontario, Canada. Since 1992, he has been a member of the Palestinian delegation to the Refugee Working Group of the multilateral track of the Middle East peace talks. He is currently completing a study of Palestinian returnees to the West Bank and is coediting an analytic bibliography on Palestinian refugees.

Preface

So far, the Middle East peace process which began in October 1991 in Madrid has yielded three agreements between the Palestinians and Israelis: the Declaration of Principles, also known as Oslo I, signed in Washington in September 1993; the Gaza-Jericho Agreement, signed in Cairo in May 1994; and an interim agreement, known as Oslo II, concluded in Washington in September 1995. The pace of translating these agreements into concrete results has been rather slow, and the outcome has been mixed for some and disappointing for others. Transfer of authority to the Palestinians has taken place in almost thirty administrative spheres, including education, health, taxation, industry and banking, tourism, telecommunications, justice, and police. Moreover, Israeli forces have been redeployed from major Palestinian towns, except for Hebron, where they continue to have a limited presence because of the Jewish settlers in the center of the city. The Palestinians elected a legislative council at the end of January 1996.

Yet developments from February to May 1996 exposed the inherent weaknesses and the asymmetry of power embedded in the three agreements. Expression of discontent with the agreements ranged from street demonstrations to attacks against Israel. In the wake of a series of suicide bombings by Hamas in Israel proper, Israel reinstituted closure of the territories, curfews, collective arrests and imprisonment, and house demolitions. Shimon Peres, who took over as prime minister following Yitzhak Rabin's assassination in November 1995, authorized sustained bombing assaults on targets deep inside Lebanon in reaction to attacks by Hizballah in northern Israel and especially against Israeli forces in the self-declared "security zone." In the eyes of the Palestinians, these and other developments rendered the agreements between them and Israel meaningless. However, the final blow to an immediate resumption of the final status talks, which had opened on 5 May 1996, was the election of Benjamin Netanyahu as Israel's prime minister and the formation of a

Likud-led government. By rejecting publicly the right of return for Palestinian refugees, the creation of a Palestinian state, withdrawal from the occupied territories, and any negotiations over the status of Jerusalem, Netanyahu's Likud has in effect rejected the Oslo agreements, which were premised on the exchange of conquered Arab land for peace.

The purpose of this study is to provide background information concerning Palestinian refugees in several areas of direct relevance for the upcoming permanent status negotiations. The objective is not to dwell on the tragic circumstances surrounding Palestinian dispersal from the homeland in 1948 and again in 1967 but to delineate the main policy and informational components of what lies behind various perceptions and definitions of the refugee issue.

Chapter 1 assembles historical and contemporary data on Palestinian refugees and places the discussion in the context of the current legal and social science literature on refugees. The purpose here is to estimate the size of the various categories of refugee and displaced populations and to underscore the specificity of the Palestinian refugee experience. In particular, it highlights the relevance of United Nations General Assembly Resolution 194(III), which stipulated options of compensation and return of the refugees.

Chapter 2 provides an understanding of the environment in which the refugees live by analyzing their legal status in the Arab host countries and by dealing, through case studies, with the socioeconomic conditions of the Palestinians living in those countries. The chapter concludes with an examination of refugees' perceptions of recent developments surrounding the peace process.

Chapter 3 outlines Israeli perceptions of the refugee issue since 1948, summarizing both official and nonofficial treatment of the right of return, compensation, and resettlement. The thrust of the chapter is to explore recent Israeli thinking on the subject, as developed by economists, lawyers, military strategists, and social scientists.

Palestinian attitudes toward the right of return, compensation, and resettlement are recounted in chapter 4. Chapter 5 examines other writings on the subject by scholars who are neither Israelis nor Palestinians but whose conclusions tend to lean in favor of either Palestinian or Israeli positions.

Finally, an attempt is made in chapter 6 to provide a synthesis of the material presented. The objective is not to reconcile differing points of view, but to arrive at a list of recommendations and policy implications that primarily serve the interests of the refugees while simultaneously contributing toward a just resolution of the Palestinian-Israeli conflict.

Two factors prompted me to undertake this project. First, my membership in the Palestinian delegation to the multilateral Refugee Working Group sensitized me to the need to assemble reliable information bearing on the complex issue of Palestinian refugees. Certainly, politics and justice do not always coincide, but whereas information does not guarantee justice for the refugees, the lack of it guarantees that politics will override justice. Second, the burgeoning field of refugee studies touches on race and ethnic relations, a subject that I research and teach and in which I am very interested. For these reasons, turning my attention to a study of Palestinian refugees was doubly rewarding.

The sheer volume of work on Palestinian refugees that is currently being carried out by research institutes, individual academics, and advocacy think tanks, not to mention international research organizations such as the United Nations and its various specialized agencies and the World Bank, is enough to intimidate the seasoned specialist. Research centers engaged in studying Palestinian refugees include no less than twenty institutions, such as the Rand Corporation, Harvard University, Yarmuk University in Jordan, Bir Zeit University in the West Bank, Tel-Aviv University, Oxford University, the Canadian International Development Agency, the Royal Institute for International Affairs in London, and the Norwegian Institute for Applied Social Science.

I have tried to synthesize in this monograph what I consider to be key studies of Palestinian refugees, relying on some seminal but mostly on recent work. I have been fortunate to spend my six-month sabbatical from teaching in the winter of 1995 in East Jerusalem at the Institute for Jerusalem Studies, whose director, Dr. Salim Tamari, provided me with the needed space to pursue my work. The Institute acted as a magnet for interesting sojourners, local as well as international, many of whom had useful things to say. I am also grateful to my students at Bir Zeit University, where I experimented with teaching a course on the sociology of refugees.

The presentation of this research is possible thanks to an invitation from the Institute of Palestine Studies to attend two seminars in London as part of a seminar series organized by the Institute on the final status issues in the Middle East peace talks. I learned a great deal from these intensive seminars, for which I am thankful.

I extend special thanks to Lex Takkenberg for making his doctoral dissertation in progress available to me, Abir Al-Bakr, Blandine Destremau, Majida Fadili, Khaled Farraj, Hunaida Ghanem, and Nabil Saleh for their invaluable assistance in preparing this study.

I owe special thanks to Nasra Hassan of UNRWA Headquarters in Vienna and Mona Nsouli of the Institute for Palestine Studies in Beirut. Their willingness to respond to desperate calls in search of references and other material made my task much easier.

Finally, I take this opportunity to express my appreciation and thanks to colleagues at the Institute for Palestine Studies in Washington, DC, in particular to Linda Butler, who always asks the right questions, and to Mark Mechler and Oliver Wilcox for their painstaking editorial work on the manuscript.

I am solely responsible for the views expressed here. Should the readers share my perspective, I would be gratified, but if the study challenges their views I would be doubly gratified. But, above all, I hope that the analysis and the implications drawn from this study contribute, even if in small measure, to rectifying the gross injustice done to the refugees of Palestine.

Elia Zureik
Kingston, Ontario, Canada
May 1996

1 | The Refugees: An Overview

Refugee Definitions and the Palestinians

Refugees and Immigrants

As a discipline, refugee studies is of a recent vintage and very much influenced by the more established tradition of migration studies. Analysis of (voluntary) migration tends to focus on individuals rather than groups. To the extent that groups are considered, they are treated as aggregates of individuals rather than as cohesive social units in the sociological sense of constituting communities with shared common historical experiences (Shami 1993). In contrast with immigrant status, refugee status is the outcome of involuntary forms of migration, in which displacement is often caused by events beyond the control of refugees, such as internal and external wars, state policies of expulsion and exclusion, development projects, and natural disasters.

Although it is customary to think of refugees and immigrants as hapless people (and to a very large extent they are), it is equally important to credit them with the ability to navigate through difficult circumstances and to construct a new suitable social world. Acknowledging the nexus between constraining and empowering aspects of the immigrant's life, Richmond (1994, 66-71) distinguished between reactive and proactive migrations depending on the immigrants' freedom of action in making decisions to migrate. *Reactive immigrants* are immigrants whose decision making is constrained, whereas *proactive immigrants* are distinguished by their relative freedom in shaping the circumstances of their relocation. Refugees may be defined as reactive immigrants, but we use the more commonly accepted term *refugee*, instead of *involuntary* or *reactive immigrant*, to refer to forced or involuntary migration.

In addition to the primary category of political refugees, the current definition of *refugee* has been widened to include economic refugees whose displacement may be caused by government economic and development policies, ecological and natural disasters, and psychological coercion. Historically, the tendency has been to label as refugees only those who are forced to leave their country, but recent definitions of refugees include internally displaced individuals as well. Anthony Richmond (1994, 67-70) identified no less than twenty-five types of refugees whose external and internal displacement has been caused by one or more of five possible factors: political, economic, environmental, social, and psychobiological.

An estimated one of every five immigrants on the move is a refugee. Excluding the most recent mass exodus of Rwandan refugees and the displacement of large numbers of people in the ongoing conflict in the Balkans, rough estimates put the number of refugees worldwide in the early 1990s at 18 million (Willigen 1993, 176). Eleven million of those refugees originated from the Middle East, Afghanistan, Ethiopia, Somalia, and other third world countries (Humphrey 1993, 2). The Gulf War alone produced in its initial phase 5 million refugees, including internal refugees in Iraq, those expelled from Kuwait (including more than 300,000 Palestinians and Jordanians), plus 800,000 Yemeni workers who were expelled by Saudi Arabia (Miller 16 June 1991, E3).

The number of refugees is substantially larger if we adopt the wider definition of refugees. A recent World Bank study put the number of people displaced as a result of so-called development projects (such as dam construction, clearing of forests, mining, and hydropower projects) in the last decade at approximately 100 million, a figure that far exceeds the current number of refugees worldwide, estimated at about 20 million (Cernea 1995).

Legal Framework

The legal framework for defining a refugee is influenced by the cold war and subsequent human migrations from the third world to the developed countries. Refugee status in the post-World War II period has been linked to human suffering and the need to provide individuals with places of residence other than their own countries on account of war, internal conflict, fear of persecution, and general instability in the countries of origin. This is the basis of refugee identification as it appears in the 1950 Statute of the Office of the United Nations High Commissioner for Refugees (UNHCR), the 1951 Refugee Convention, and the 1967 United Nations Refugee Protocol.

Other sources for defining a refugee may be found in various UN resolutions and agreements concluded by regional organizations. Early UN resolutions that identified refugee groups by name include UN General Assembly Resolution 194 (III) of 11 December 1948 (see Appendix 1), which referred to the "refugees of Palestine," and subsequent resolutions that reaffirmed it. Identification of specific groups of refugees is also reflected in the creation of agencies for dealing with such types of refugees, such as the United Nations Relief and Works Agency (UNRWA), established in late 1949 to cater exclusively to Palestinian refugees, and the United Nations Korean Reconstruction Agency, established in the wake of the Korean war.

Definitions of the term *refugee* are also provided by regional organizations. Hathaway (1991, 16) cited Article 1, paragraph 2 of the 1969 Organization of African Unity Convention:

> The term refugee shall also apply to every person who, owing to external aggression, occupation, foreign domination or events seriously disturbing public order in either part or the whole of his country of origin or nationality, is compelled to leave his place of national habitat in order to seek refuge in another place outside his country of origin or nationality. (p. 16)

The Covenant of Europe Definition of Refugee Status concentrates on those who are "unable or unwilling for . . . varied reasons to return to their countries of origin" (cited in Hathaway 1991, 21). The Organization of American States in its 1985 Cartagena Declaration defined *refugees* in a manner similar to that provided by the Organization of African Unity. The Arab League Charter singled out Palestinian refugees for special consideration by guaranteeing them equal treatment and freedom of movement in the host countries without prejudicing their right of return. (Chapter 2 demonstrates, however, that the status of Palestinian refugees in Arab countries is far from being uniformly defined as stipulated in the League's Charter.)

The thrust of refugee law in the aftermath of World War II has been not so much on repatriation but on compensation and providing new places of residence for displaced people (i.e., resettlement) and recognizing the need to protect such individuals from persecution either in their adopted countries or in their countries of origin, should they be forced or choose to return to them. These are the parameters that continue to inform current debates on refugees and immigrants.

Defining the Palestinian Refugee

The question of Palestinian refugees predates by almost half a century the current debates about refugees in general. It is no exaggeration to say that it has been the most intractable issue to face the international community since World War II. No thorough understanding of the Palestinian refugee case is possible without fully appreciating the environment in which Palestinian refugees live and the attitudes of the international community, the Israeli government, and the Palestinians themselves.

Contrary to the thrust of refugee law, which deals with compensation and resettlement, the emphasis in the Palestinian case is on repatriation to their country of origin. The main wish of Palestinian refugees is to be allowed to return to their homeland. Lex Takkenberg (1995) expressed this situation succinctly:

> An essential feature of refugeehood is that it concerns people who have left their country--either that of their nationality or in case of stateless people that of their former habitual residence--out of fear for persecution, and who are *unable*, or, owing to such fear, are *unwilling* to return to it . . . . In the case of Palestine refugees it is generally the opposite. The vast majority of Palestine refugees have expressed their willingness to return to their country. (p. 3; emphasis in original)

Although Radley (1978) did not interpret international law as sanctioning the repatriation of Palestinian refugees, he nevertheless concurred that Palestinian refugees are unique "in their desire to return to their country of origin while the general political conditions that caused them to become refugees persist" (p. 611). This is why Palestinians regard UN General Assembly Resolution 194 (III) as being very important. It deals specifically with Palestinian refugees and provides an option of return and payment of compensation to those whose property was damaged or those not wishing to return. The drawback of the specific designation of Palestinian refugees as UNRWA's sole responsibility is that they are excluded from human rights protection accorded to refugees who fall under the umbrella of the UNHCR and other international bodies (Takkenberg 1991, 421; Raei 1995).

According to UNRWA, "Palestine refugees" and their descendants "shall mean any person whose normal place of residence was Palestine during the period 1 June 1946 to 15 May 1948 and who lost both his home and means of livelihood as a result of the 1948 conflict" (UN document, Consolidated Eligibility Instructions, document Rev. 7/83, January 1984). Generally, this remains the accepted operational definition of Palestinian refugees. However, Palestinian refugees include categories of displaced individuals who fall outside UNRWA's responsibility and definition. These include:

• Palestinian refugees from the 1948 war who ended up in places other than UNRWA's area of operations, i.e., Egypt and other North African countries, Iraq, and the Gulf region;

• Internally displaced Palestinians, who remained in the area that became Israel and were originally acknowledged as UNRWA's responsibility but who were subsequently excluded on the assumption that their condition would be addressed by Israel;

• Residents from Gaza and the West Bank (including East Jerusalem) and their descendants, who were displaced for the first time in the 1967 war;

• Individuals who, after 1967, were deported by the Israeli occupation authorities from the West Bank and Gaza;

• So-called "late comers," i.e., those who left the occupied territories to study, visit relatives, work, get married, etc., whose Israeli-issued residency permits expired and who were prevented by Israel from returning to their homes;

• Palestinians who were outside British Mandatory Palestine when the 1948 war broke out, or those who were outside the territories when the 1967 war broke out and who were prevented from returning by Israel; and

• Well-to-do Palestinians who sought refuge in 1948 but whose pride prevented them from registering with UNRWA.

Our definition of refugees and displaced Palestinians is consistent with the following definition provided in the statement of the Palestinian delegation at the first meeting of the Refugee Working Group (RWG) held in Ottawa, Canada on 13 May 1992:

The Palestinian refugees are all those Palestinians (and their descendants) who were expelled or forced to leave their homes between November 1947 (Partition Plan) and January 1949 (Rhodes Armistice Agreements), from the territory controlled by Israel on that latter date. This . . . coincides with the Israeli definition of absentees, a category of Palestinians meant to be stripped of its most elementary human and civil rights:

Any person was declared to be an absentee if he was, on, or after 29th November 1947 a citizen or a subject of any of the Arab states; in any of these states for any length of time in any part of Palestine outside the Israeli-occupied area, or in any place other than his habitual residence even if such place as well as his habitual abode were within Israeli-occupied territory.

This definition does not only apply to camp-dwellers, and certainly not only to those recognized refugees who enjoyed formal registration by UNRWA, since the latter never exercised jurisdiction over more than a segment of the total refugee population

Such a definition does not include emigrants who left Palestine before 1947, but it includes all those displaced, even inside the territory that became the State of Israel in the 1948-49 period. It also includes all the 1967 and post-1967 displaced persons . . . .

It also includes the residents of "border villages" in the West Bank, who lost their agricultural lands in the war of 1948, and therefore the source of their livelihood, but remained in their villages. It includes residents of the Gaza Strip refugee camps who were either relocated in the Rafah side of the Egyptian boundary, or who found themselves separated from their families and kin as a result of border demarcation after the Camp David Agreement between Israel and Egypt. It finally includes Palestinian Bedouins who were forcibly removed from their grazing lands within the State of Israel, as well as those who were induced to abandon the West Bank and to relocate in Jordan.

Although some of the above categories may not be regarded as refugees in the technical sense (for example deportees, or residents of "border villages"), they nevertheless share the hardships and fate of most refugees who fall in the first categories. At the core of their status is land alienation and the denial of return to their country. (Statement 1992, 5-6; emphasis in original)

Refugees and the Peace Process

The Middle East Peace Conference, convened in Madrid by the United States and USSR in the fall of 1991, set up a two-tiered peace process: a bilateral track of negotiations between Israel and each of its neighbors and a multilateral track consisting of five working groups dealing with issues of security, refugees, economy, the environment, and water. The main objective of these groups was to exchange technical information while at the same time building mutual confidence among the parties concerned and preparing the ground for anticipated political negotiations.

As of late 1991, then, the question of the Palestinian refugees has been the subject of discussion of the RWG on this multilateral track. As envisaged by the sponsors, the work of the RWG is basically technical and intended to suggest practical solutions that will feed into future bilateral negotiations. During the eight RWG meetings held as of May 1996, and several intersessional gatherings, discussions have focused on ameliorating the conditions of the refugees in their dispersed communities. Programs of a humanitarian and practical nature have been introduced, with the European Union (EU) taking the lead in the development of social and economic infrastructure, France concerning itself with family reunification projects, Italy with public health, Norway with data bases, Sweden with child welfare, and the U.S. with human resource development, vocational training, and job creation. More recently, in December 1995, Switzerland agreed to shepherd an additional theme having to do with civil and human rights.

After four years, the RWG, with Canada as its gavelholder, has been able to show progress on several fronts, such as funding research and carrying out feasibility studies on various aspects of refugee life, but little has been achieved by way of concrete results with regard to the main issue on its agenda, that of family reunification.

The Declaration of Principles (DOP), signed by Israel and the PLO in 1993, allows for additional discussion of the Palestine refugee issue on two levels. The 1967 refugees, the so-called displaced persons, are being discussed through a Quadripartite Committee composed of Palestinians, Egyptians, Israelis, and Jordanians. The 1948 refugees are supposed to be discussed during the bilateral final status talks between Palestinians and Israelis, which officially began in May 1996 but were stalled after the recent Israeli elections.

The Madrid peace process and the DOP are anchored in UN Security Council Resolutions 242 and 338, adopted following the 1967 and 1973 Arab-Israeli wars, respectively. Both resolutions fall short of recognizing Palestinian national rights. The fate of the 1948 refugees is particularly handicapped by the absence of any direct reference to the seminal General Assembly Resolution 194 (III) of 11 December 1948 (see Appendix 2).

Estimates of the Palestinian Population

The West Bank and Gaza

Recent estimates of the Palestinian population in the West Bank (including East Jerusalem) and Gaza carried out by the U.S. Census Bureau and the Palestine Central Bureau of Statistics show that for 1995 the combined population of the territories stood at 2,390,000, with 1,485,000 living in the West Bank (including East Jerusalem) and 905,000 in Gaza. During the last four years, immigration into the territories has outstripped emigration. In light of the unfolding peace process, it is assumed that, in addition to natural increase, some 250,000 Palestinians will return to the territories between 1994 and 1999. If this immigration materializes, it is projected that the Palestinian population of the occupied territories may reach 4,650,000 by the year 2012. Without this immigration, the total population of the territories is expected to reach 4,235,000 (Adlakha, Kinsella, and Khawaja 1995).

Although no official estimates exist regarding the probable number of Palestinian returnees, Israeli analyst Zvit Steinboim (1993, 37-38) estimated that 1 million people will go back to the West Bank and Gaza during the first five years after the signing of the final agreement ending the Palestinian-Arab-Israeli conflict. This estimate is based on the economic absorptive capacity of the territories and on the extent of integration of refugees in host countries. Steinboim estimated that some 150,000 would choose to come back from Jordan and only a very small number--those co-opted by the Palestinian leadership to join the emerging Palestinian administration--from Egypt. Among the Palestinians in Syria, she estimated that 50,000-80,000 would return, as would most of Lebanon's 300,000 Palestinians. Writing before the huge Palestinian exodus from the Gulf countries in the wake of the 1991 Gulf War, Steinboim estimated that half of the 750,000 Palestinians living in the Gulf would return. Of those living in North America, Europe, and other parts of the world, a mere 50,000-100,000 would return for ideological reasons.

Global Estimates

A U.S. Census Bureau study estimated that 6,450,000 Palestinians live in the sixteen Middle Eastern and North African countries (Adlakha, Kinsclla, and Khawaja 1995, 8; Tables 1 and 8). When the half million or so Palestinians living outside the Middle East and North Africa are added, the global estimate of the Palestinian population reached 7 million in the mid-1990s (see also Kossaifi 1996, 2). This is slightly higher than the figures published by the Israeli newspaper *Ha'Aretz* on 21 July 1995, as shown in Table 1. The latter underestimates the Palestinian population in each of Egypt, Syria, Europe, and the Americas and overestimates the number of Palestinians in Lebanon.

Using data from sixteen countries, Kinsella (1991, 57) calculated that the number of Palestinians in the Middle East and North Africa will reach around 9.4 million by the year 2010. Adding the number of Palestinians in Europe and the Americas would bring the total Palestinian population worldwide to more than 10 million by 2010.

Arab-Jewish Population Balance

Table 2 gives a projection over the next decade of the Arab-Jewish population balance in what was Mandatory Palestine (see map in Appendix 1). The projection is based on three assumptions for the period covered: that current rates of natural increase for both Arabs and Jews will continue; that some 250,000 Palestinians will return to the occupied

Table 1

Distribution of the Palestinian Population
Worldwide, 1995

Place of Residence	Population[a]
West Bank	1,116,228
Gaza	700,000
Israel	770,652
Jordan	2,000,000
Lebanon	480,643
Syria	302,587
Iraq	50,257
Egypt	72,154
Kuwait	75,000
Saudi Arabia	181,787
Gulf states	66,853
Libya	24,438
Europe and the Americas	388,437
Total	6,409,036

Source: *Ha'Aretz*, 21 July 1995.

[a]Population includes those who are registered refugees as well as those who do not appear in the UNWRA register.

Table 2
Projected Arab and Jewish Population in the Area
of Former Mandate Palestine,
1992-2005 (in thousands)

Year	Arabs[a]	Jews[b]
1992	2,800	4,189
1995	3,255	4,662
2000	4,125	4,837
2005	4,848	5,002

[a] For the population projections of the occupied territories, including East Jerusalem, see Adlakha, Kinsella, and Khawajah, 1995, Table 8 and Appendix, p. 1. The Arab population estimates of the occupied territories were added to the Palestinian population of Israel, minus the Arab population of East Jerusalem (in order to avoid counting of East Jerusalem's Arab population twice).

The 1992 population estimates and projections of the Arab population in Israel were taken from *Statistical Abstract of Israel*, No. 44, 1993, p. 43 for 1992, and pp. 92-93 for the years 1995, 2000, and 2005; the projections for the Arab population of East Jerusalem for 1995, 2000, and 2005 were taken from *Statistical Yearbook of Jerusalem*, No. 11, 1994, p. 29.

[b] Projections for the Jewish population are taken from *Statistical Abstract of Israel*, No. 44, 1993, pp. 92-93.

territories between 1994 and 1999; and that some 500,000 Jews will immigrate from the former Soviet Union. On such a basis, parity will be reached by the year 2005 between the Palestinian population and the Jewish population in historic Palestine. If, however, the number of Palestinian returnees from the 1967 war reaches 500,000 or more, as expected by some Palestinian planners (*Program for Development of the Palestinian National Economy for the Years 1994-2000*, 1993) and if further large-scale Jewish immigration from Russia and elsewhere to Israel does not materialize, the population balance may tip in the Palestinians' favor.

Distribution of the Refugee Population

Although a discussion of the circumstances surrounding the creation of the Palestinian refugee problem in 1948 is beyond the scope of this study, the magnitude of the exodus is quite pertinent. Table 3 presents various estimates of the initial dispersal in 1948--that is, the core group of what later became known as the refugees of Palestine. The UNRWA estimate of 1949 provides the base for an ongoing count of the refugee population registered with the agency, although, as we show elsewhere in this study, this figure is by no means comprehensive.

As for the current number of Palestinian refugees, Table 4 presents UNRWA's latest figures, which show 3,093,174 Palestinian refugees registered with the agency in early 1995, distributed regionally as follows: 40 percent in Jordan; 38 percent in the West Bank and Gaza; and about 11 percent each in Syria and Lebanon.

Table 4 shows that the registered refugee population in early 1995 constitutes slightly less than half of the estimated 6.5 million Palestinians worldwide, or about the same proportion as at the time of the 1948 dispersal. It should be noted that UNRWA's definition of refugees is necessarily restricted to those receiving its aid. In a broader sense, all those who left in 1948 are refugees. Thus, UNRWA figures are a good start, but there is no way of knowing exactly how many refugees there are short of a complete census of the Palestinians worldwide. Some writers claim that the UNRWA figures exaggerate the number of refugees because accurate statistics of deaths are not maintained (Efrat 1993). Although there is some truth in this claim, it is equally possible that there is an undercount of the total displaced Palestinian population, which according to UNRWA amounts to 12 percent of Palestinian refugees

Table 3
Estimates of Refugees According to Areas of Arrival
1948-1949

Areas of Arrival	Official British Estimates	Official U.S. Estimates	United Nations Estimates	Private Israeli Estimates	Official Israeli Estimates	Palestinian Estimates
Gaza	210,000	208,000	280,000	200,000		201,173
West Bank	320,000		190,000	200,000		363,689
Arab countries	280,000	667,000	256,000	250,000		284,324
Totals	810,000[a]	875,000[b]	726,000[c]	650,000	520,000[f]	849,186[h]
			957,000[c]	600,000-700,000[d]	590,000[g]	714,150-744,150[i]
				620,000[e]		770,100-780,000[j]

[a]See document from PRO FO371/754196 E2297/1821/31, in Morris 1987, pp. 297, 364. Estimate as of February 1949.
[b]"The Problem of Arab Refugees from Palestine." The West Bank refugees are added to those of Jordan. Estimate as of 1953.
[c]United Nations Conciliation Commission for Palestine, p. 18; United Nations. *Annual Report of the Director General of UNRWA*, Doc.5224/5223, 25 November 1952. First estimate as of September 1949; second estimate as of May 1950.
[d]Morris 1990, p. 68. Estimates as of 1948-1950
[e] Efrat 1993. Estimate as of mid-1949.
[f] Morris 1987, p. 297. Estimate as of 1948.
[g] The estimate is as of 1992, based on a report by the Israeli Foreign Ministry, published in *al-Quds*, 10 September 1992.
[h] Hagopian and Zahlan, p. 53. Estimate as of November 1952.
[i] W. Khalidi 1992, Appendix III, p. 582. Estimate as of mid-1948.
[j] Edward Said et al 1990, p. 6; J. Abu-Lughod 1971, pp. 139-63. Estimate as of late 1948.

Table 4
Distribution of UNRWA-Registered Palestinian Refugees, 1995

	Lebanon	Syria	Jordan	Gaza	West Bank	Total
Registered refugees	342,121	332,465	1,239,811	666,343	512,434	3,093,174
Percentage of annual increase	2.2	3.4	7.6	6.0	4.9	5.5
Percentage of country population	11.6	2.4	30.3	76.2	36.7	13.4
Percentage of refugee distribution	11.1	10.7	40.1	21.5	16.6	100
Number of refugee camps	12	13	10	8	19	62
Percentage of refugees in camps	52.3	27.9	20.0	55.7	25.7	33.1

Source: UNRWA General Information Sheet, Program Planning and Evaluation Office. Amman, Jordan, January 1995.

(Artz 1996). Several factors contribute to a possible refugee undercount. First, the 1948 armistice line split several Palestinian border villages in the West Bank and Gaza and denied Bedouin access to their grazing lands. Altogether some 300,000 people were affected who did not come under UNRWA's jurisdiction, even though for all intents and purposes they were refugees (Peretz 1995; B. Schiff 1995). Second, UNRWA-registered refugees do not include stateless Palestinians in places where UNRWA does not operate, such as Egypt, North Africa, Iraq, and the Gulf countries. Third, middle-class Palestinians who became refugees in 1948 did not register with UNRWA, nor did those who acquired citizenship either in the Arab world (mainly Jordan) or outside it. Fourth, the offspring of refugee women who marry nonrefugees lose their refugee status with UNRWA (Cervenak 1994).

It is interesting to note in this regard that a consequence of the Gulf War and the Oslo agreement has been a rush by Palestinians to reclaim their refugee status. According to UNRWA sources, the largest increase in refugee registration in 1994 was due to the Gulf War and not to natural increase. Two factors account for this: The Gulf War contributed to the impoverishment of Palestinians who were settled in the Gulf and who became destitute after their expulsion from the region, and speculation about refugee compensation upon reaching a final settlement of the conflict has driven members of displaced Palestinian communities to come forward and reactivate their refugee status and claims. A similar point is made by Kossaifi (1996, 5) who notes that the Palestinian refugee population has increased in 1990-95 by 5.4 percent, which is nearly twice the rate of natural increase experienced between 1985 and 1995. The latter increase is due mainly to the activated refugee status by Gulf returnees.

In addition to the refugee population referred to above, close to 20 percent of the Palestinian population in Israel proper (i.e., 120,000-150,000) consists of internal refugees who were displaced from their villages in 1948 and who were not allowed to go back to their homes (Al-Haj 1991, 246). They are demanding that their case be resolved in any final settlement reached between the Palestinians and Israelis; increasingly, their cause is receiving publicity both inside and outside Israel. In March 1995, they aired their grievances at a conference organized by the Committee for the Defense of the Rights of Refugees in Israel, attended by 300 representatives from 40 uprooted villages within Israel proper (Ashkar 1995, 17).

Strictly speaking, UNRWA's mandate does not extend to those who became refugees for the first time as a result of the 1967 war (referred to as "displaced persons" in the parlance of the current discussion of the Quadripartite Committee of the Middle East peace talks), but UNRWA contributes to their well-being in conjunction with the host governments (primarily Jordan and Syria). Some of those who became refugees in 1948 settled in camps in Gaza and the West Bank and subsequently found themselves refugees for the second time in 1967. These people remain UNRWA's responsibility and are included in the above statistics.

According to UNRWA (1992, *Family Reunification*), 350,000 people (encompassing first- and second-time refugees and originating from the West Bank, Gaza, and the Golan Heights) were displaced during the 1967 war and ended up in Jordan, Syria, and Egypt. About 5,000 proceeded to Lebanon. UNRWA's breakdown of the figures is as follows: (1) 200,000, including 93,000 UNRWA-registered refugees, went to Jordan from the occupied territories; (2) 110,000, including 70,000 UNRWA-registered refugees, fled the Golan Heights to camps near Damascus and Dar'a; and (3) 35,000, including 3,000 UNRWA-registered refugees, crossed the Suez Canal into Egypt. An additional 3,000-4,000 Palestinian youth were forced by the Israelis to leave Gaza to Egypt under the pretext that they were members of the Palestine Liberation Army.

A similar account of the impact of the 1967 war on population displacement has been given by Lex Takkenberg (1991), a lawyer and an UNRWA official:

> the [1948] Refugees in Southern Syria were displaced for the second time when Israeli forces occupied the Golan Heights and the Quneitra area. Many moved towards Damascus and to Dar'a further south. About 150,000 registered refugees from the West Bank and some 38,500 refugees from the Gaza Strip fled to east Jordan, where they were joined by another 200,000 non-refugee former residents of the West Bank and Gaza Strip, fleeing for the first time. (p. 420)

Brand (1994, 52) stated that 250,000 refugees crossed from the West Bank to east Jordan in 1967.

At a recent conference on family reunification held in Ramallah on 18 November 1995, a member of the Palestinian delegation of the RWG and the Quadripartite Committee ('Amro 1995) presented data on people displaced as a result of the 1967 war (see Table 5). His total of 413,160

Table 5
Palestinian Estimates of Displaced Persons and Refugees
During the 1967 War

Category	Estimate
Displaced to Jordan	
1967 Displaced persons for the first time	107,000
1948 Refugees displaced for the second time	93,000
Unclear status (inlcuding residents of three Latroun villages near Jerusalem)	12,500
Total	212,500
Displaced to Egypt	
1967 Displaced persons for the first time	32,000
1948 Refugees displaced for the second time	3,000
Deportees	4,000
Total	39,000
People abroad who were unable to or prevented from return	60,000
Persons with "lost ID" permits (1967-91)	100,000[a]
Deportees (1967-91)	1,660[b]
Total	413,160

Source: 'Amro 1995.

[a] Equivalent to the 54,000 permits according to Jordanian figures.
[b] According to Jordanian figures. This figure does not include dependents who might have joined the deportees at a later time.

displaced by the 1967 war initially appears at odds with UNWRA's estimate of 350,000. However, the cause of the discrepancy lies primarily in his inclusion of 60,000 residents of the territories who were abroad when the 1967 war broke out and who were not allowed to return, a category not included in UNWRA's figures. When this difference is accounted for, the estimates are very close.

As shown in Table 6, official Jordanian estimates of the 1967 displaced persons and refugees, including latecomers, deportees, descendants, and considering natural growth, put the number in 1994 at more than 1 million (Jaber 1996).

After the first meeting of the Quadripartite Committee in Amman on 7 March 1995, Israeli delegate Shlomo Gazit published various categories of Palestinians that, according to Israel, qualify for discussion by that committee (cited in Takkenberg 1995, 24): "(1) residents of the territories who fled to the East Bank of the Jordan River with the retreating Jordanian army; (2) residents who moved east of the Jordan River in the second half of 1967. Most of these were women, children, and old people joining family members on the East Bank (and a few in Egypt) whose return to the West Bank and Gaza Strip was prevented by the Israel Defense Forces (IDF); (3) residents who were working, studying, or otherwise away from their homes when the IDF occupied the area; and (4) residents who left the area in subsequent years, but missed the return deadline stated on their exit permits and have since been prevented from returning." It should be noted that Israel, in addition to using the low figure of 200,000 persons displaced by the 1967 war (Nir 1995), also rejects out of hand the notion that the descendants of those displaced should be allowed to return to the territories. The Arab figures, on the other hand, begin with an estimate closer to 400,000 for those actually displaced as a result of the 1967 war and include their descendants, which brings the total to about 800,000.

Disagreement over numbers is only one of the many problems facing Palestinian and Arab negotiators in their dealings with the issue of family reunification. The number of those people allowed to return by Israel is small. According to UNRWA (1992a, 11), 85,163 applications for family reunification were presented by the Palestinians to Israeli authorities between 1967 and 1987, and 12,814 (i.e., 15%) of them were approved by Israel; 3,226 applications for family reunification were submitted between 1987 and 1989, of which 695 (i.e., about 20%) were approved. Between 1968 and 1994, Israeli sources quoted by Gazit (1994b) state

Table 6
Official Jordanian Estimates of
Displaced Palestinians and Refugees

Category	1967 Estimates	1994 Estimates
Displaced refugees		
From the West Bank	150,000	452,412
From Gaza	38,500	78,786
Total	188,500	531,198
Displaced persons		
From the West Bank	178,000	444,927
From Gaza	22,000	55,490
Total	200,000	500,417
Displaced persons carrying Israeli permits (Latecomers)		
From the West Bank		39,440
From Gaza		48,771
Total		88,211
Deportees		12,500
Total	388,500	1,132,326

Source: Jaber 1996.

that 88,000 people were allowed into the West Bank on a humanitarian basis under the family reunification scheme. This figure excludes 20,000 people who were admitted as members of the Palestinian police force and their dependents, most of whom went to Gaza, but it probably includes the 14,000 people Israel admitted back immediately after the 1967 war between the end of June and the end of August 1967, and an additional 4,000 who were admitted between September 1967 and 30 June 1968.

If one accepts for the sake of argument the figure of 88,000 and pro-rates it over a twenty-seven-year period (from 1967 to 1994), then Israel allowed, on average, 3,251 people to return per year. If this is the rate at which Israel intends to operate, then it would take over sixty years to allow the return of the minimum number of 200,000 displaced persons by Israeli calculations (Nir 1995), and more than two centuries to absorb the estimated Arab figure of 800,000! Since August 1994, as a result of discussions in the multilateral negotiations, Israel promised to entertain the return of 2,000 family reunification cases per year, each case being assumed to involve about four persons. By June 1995, it had admitted close to 80 percent of this number, or about 6,000 persons. If calculations are made on the basis of 6,000 per year, then it would take thirty-three years to bring back the original 200,000 refugees, which Israel purports to be the number of displaced Palestinians in 1967. In the absence of agreed upon and clear criteria involving international monitoring and transparency of procedures, it is difficult to verify the progress of refugee admissions, which are minuscule by any standards. Furthermore, the above discussion does not address the fate of the 1948 refugees, who form the bulk of the more than 3 million refugees registered with UNRWA. Thus, the reader may get a sense of the nature of the problems that refugee repatriation is likely to encounter in the coming negotiations.

The intake of Palestinian returnees has been counterbalanced by a large wave of out-migration from the territories due primarily to the lack of economic opportunities. Kossaifi estimated that between 1968 and 1986 a total of 400,000 Palestinians left the territories. Most of these are unable to return since Israel considers them "voluntary" migrants, whereas Kossaifi referred to this phenomenon as "forced migration" (1996, 7).

As a result of the 1948 war, the 1967 war, the 1970 civil war in Jordan, and the 1982 Israeli invasion of Lebanon, Palestinians moved to Kuwait and other Gulf countries. On the eve of the Gulf War, the Palestinian-Jordanian population numbered between 350,000 and 400,000 in Kuwait alone. Most of them were expelled from Kuwait in the aftermath of the Gulf War, except for some 30,000 who were allowed to stay. Of those who were expelled, a few thousand went to Iraq, about 30,000 returned to the West Bank, and the rest went to Jordan.

The most vulnerable group of Palestinian refugees are the close to 70,000 refugees who fled in 1967 from Gaza to Jordan and found their way to other parts of the Middle East, mainly to the Gulf region. These refugees are not covered by any specific international protection, and they lack documents to facilitate their movement across international boundaries, as became apparent after the Gulf War (Gilen et al. 1994, 23). They hold (expired) Egyptian travel documents, and Egypt has not permitted their return or the renewal of their documents. Even if they were permitted to return to Egypt, however, they would not be covered by UNRWA's assistance program because Egypt is not considered an UNRWA area of operation (Takkenberg 1995, chapter 3). Similar difficulties are faced by those Palestinian refugees in Lebanon who leave the country at the risk of losing their residency rights, and thus becoming stateless without any international protection. It is ironic that, just as the issue of Palestinian refugees is about to be discussed in the context of a final settlement between the Palestinians and Israelis, a new refugee camp has sprung up in North Africa on the border between Libya and Egypt as a result of Libya's expulsion of its Palestinian population (*al-Hayat*, 5 October 1995).

Table 7 summarizes data on the 1948 Palestinian refugees, the 1967 displaced Palestinians, latecomers, deportees, and internally displaced Palestinians in Israel. Close to 4 million Palestinians can be classified as refugees and displaced persons.

The 1995 figure of close to 4 million registered refugees and displaced Palestinians, given in Table 7, is more than twice the figure reached by Israeli researcher Moshe Efrat (Klinov 1995). Efrat (1976) claimed that UNRWA's original count of 835,000 refugees after the 1948 war was higher than his estimate of 604,000 by almost one-third. Furthermore, in subsequent calculations, he excluded from his figures Palestinian refugees who do not live in the camps, those who were displaced in 1967 for the first time, Palestinians who live in Egypt and other places in the Arab countries where UNRWA does not operate, latecomers, and internally displaced refugees in Israel proper. In other words, Efrat's actual (if not nominal) definition of a Palestinian refugee is someone who still lives in an UNRWA camp.

Table 7
Estimates of Palestinian Refugees and Displaced Persons, 1995

Category	Estimate
1948 Refugees (UNWRA responsibility)	3,093,174[a]
1948 Refugees (non-UNRWA responsibility)	182,355[b]
1948 Internally displaced in Israel	150,000
1967 Displaced persons (excluding 1948 refugees)	400,000[c]-500,000[d]
Latecomers/Lost IDs	88,000[e]-100,000[f]
Deportees to Egypt and Jordan	5,660[g]-12,500[h]
Total	3,919,189-4,038,029

[a] See Table 4.

[b] Egypt, Iraq, Libya, Algeria, and the remaining Palestinian population in Kuwait (see Kinsella 1991). No estimates can be made of the number of Palestinians who were left after the Gulf War in Saudi Arabia, Qatar, Oman and Bahrain, which according to the U.S. census projections, would have had 291,494 Palestinians in 1995 (Kinsella 1991).

[c] UNRWA estimates that around 350,000 Palestinians were displaced as a result of the 1967 war and that roughly half (166,000) were registered with UNRWA. These are second-time refugees. The rest were displaced for the first time. Taking into account rates of natural increase, the displaced population of 1967 was expected to double its size in twenty-eight years, to around 800,000. However, because half are second-time refugees and are counted in UNRWA's figures, this leaves around 400,000 in 1995 who may be classified as originally displaced for the first time in 1967.

[d] Based on figures in Table 6.

[e] Lower estimate, based on figures in Table 6.

[f] Table 5

[g] Table 5

[h] Table 6

From a policy perspective, this definition is unacceptable. The only acceptable definition is one that is necessarily inclusive rather than exclusive, so as to give Palestinian refugees living outside and inside former Mandatory Palestine, and inside as well as outside camps, the option of return (its modalities to be decided through negotiations), the right of compensation, and normalization of their citizenship status.

2 | Refugees in Arab States and the Occupied Territories

This chapter describes the environment in which Palestinian refugees have been living since 1948. The legal status of the refugees in the host Arab states has varied from country to country. The position of the Arab states toward the Palestine question in general, and the refugees in particular, cannot be divorced from the ongoing interplay of Arab politics in the region. In general, the situation of Palestinian refugees is adversely affected by some background features of Arab political life. The absence of democracy and an egalitarian economic order in the Arab world and the episodic flare-up of regional and ethnic conflicts which challenge the legitimacy of ruling regimes have all contributed to Arab governmental intolerance of minorities in their midst. Be it Lebanon, the Gulf countries, Jordan, or other Arab states, the Palestinians have received more than their share of blame, rightly or wrongly, for internal instability, which in turn has contributed to their precarious status.

As Laurie Brand (1988) demonstrated, the fortunes of the Palestinians in the Arab world have depended on the extent of their inclusion in or exclusion from societal participation. In societies where they were treated as marginal, nonintegrated groups and the host society was weak (e.g., Lebanon prior to the Syrian intervention and Israeli invasion in the early 1980s or Jordan before the outbreak of the civil war in the early 1970s), they tended to create parallel and separate institutions that catered to their needs. In Egypt, after the eclipse of Nasserism in the early 1970s, the Palestinians became marginalized, and the government tended to apply maximum coercive power in controlling them. Before the Gulf War, Palestinians in Kuwait were able to work and contribute to the building of the country; like other nonnationals, however, they were not allowed to become citizens, own property, or participate in political life.

Historically, three principles have shaped Arab state policies toward Palestinian refugees. First, in order to highlight the plight of the refugees and to put pressure on Israel to admit responsibility for them, Arab countries (except Jordan) have denied citizenship rights to the Palestinians in their midst; in so doing, they claimed they were serving the interests of the Palestinians and supporting their right of return. Second, on paper at least, Arab countries of first refuge adopted, as early as 1952, through the Council of Ministers of the Arab League, a series of resolutions granting Palestinian refugees residency rights and the right to work on an equal footing with citizens of member states of the League. However, the application of these legal resolutions has been uneven, to say the least. Finally, uncertainties in the status of Palestinians in the Arab countries were also a function of the PLO's attitude to the refugee question. For example, the PLO originally rejected any attempts by refugee organizations, including the UNHCR, to assist in settling Palestinian refugees in third countries (whether in the West or in Arab countries), and did not press for their rights to be normalized in the host countries for fear that this would lead to their resettlement and the loss of their collective right of return.

Legal Status

In 1964, the Arab League adopted the Casablanca Protocol, which widened the scope of Palestinian rights by granting them the freedom to travel from one country to the next and to return to the country of their residence without hindrance. A closer look at the Protocol is instructive. This seemingly liberal policy, enabling the refugees to move freely, amounted to nothing more "than a statement of good intent[, rather] than a hard commitment on the part of member states" (Takkenberg 1995, 13). Moreover, Arab governments adopted different stances toward implementing the Casablanca Protocol. In the words of one analyst,

[a] first group [of Arab countries] agreed to it without reservation (Jordan, Algeria, Sudan, Iraq, Syria, Egypt, and Yemen), a second group (Lebanon, Kuwait and Libya) agreed to it with reservations, a third group (Morocco and Saudi Arabia) did not declare its position towards it, and other states did not attend the League's meeting; yet others joined the Arab League after the signing of the Protocol, and

their [official] position remains unclear (Bahrain, Qatar, Oman, and the Arab Emirates). (Al-Aza'r 1995, 13)

Ultimately, only two states with a significant Palestinian presence, Syria and Jordan, fully ratified the Casablanca Protocol, whereas Kuwait and Lebanon never implemented its provisions. Others, such as Egypt and Libya, implemented it inconsistently.

To make matters more complicated, the protocol was never harmonized with the immigration and citizenship laws of the host states, let alone with international conventions pertaining to refugees. Whenever conflict arose between national legislation and implementation of the Casablanca Protocol, national legislation prevailed. Takkenberg noted that these formal agreements and resolutions were easily swept aside by host governments in favor of fiats and edicts, and the position of the refugees was largely dictated by prevailing political conditions. More recently, the Gulf War led most Arab states officially to suspend implementation of the protocol and to replace it with *ad hoc* state policies lacking clarity and coherence.

What complicates the picture even further is that, with the exception of Egypt, Morocco, and Tunisia, Arab countries are not signatories to the United Nations Refugee Convention of 1951 or the Refugee Protocol of 1967, which protect the rights of refugees and asylum seekers. As part of a recent drive to protect human rights in the Arab world, Arab experts met in 1991 in Cairo, the third such meeting to take place under the auspices of the UNHCR, and adopted the Declaration on the Protection of Refugees and Displaced Persons in the Arab World. The conference was attended by Arab government officials, but the recommendations of the conference were nonbinding on the governments concerned. The meeting of experts adopted a resolution which, though expansive in terms of widening refugee protection measures, remained true to the historic (inconsistent) stance regarding Palestinian refugees. In part, the resolution declared that it

> strongly emphasizes the need to ensure international protection for Palestinian refugees by competent international organizations and, in particular, by the United Nations, without in any way prejudicing the inalienable rights of the Palestinian people, especially their right to repatriation and self-determination. (cited in Takkenberg 1995, chapter 4, 4; see also Elmadmad 1993)

Immigration and naturalization laws of Arab countries are overlaid with political considerations. Whereas most countries around the world grant citizenship rights through naturalization or birth or by marriage, in Arab countries marriage of a male nonnational to a female national does not automatically entail citizenship rights for the nonnational. Likewise, as is clear to the Palestinians in Kuwait, Lebanon, Egypt, Syria, and other Arab countries, the mere fact of birth in an Arab country does not carry with it the advantages of citizenship, nor does an extended stay for purposes of work.

A country-by-country summary of the main policies governing the treatment of Palestinian refugees in the Arab host countries is presented. These policies derive from a combination of codified law, precedent, and political expediency.

Jordan

An integral part of Jordan's plan to build a nation was the granting of full citizenship rights to the Palestinian population in accordance with the 1954 Jordanian Nationality Law. This policy of integration, which followed the annexation by Jordan of the West Bank after the 1948 war, was also motivated by attempts to neutralize any challenge to the Jordanian regime from the Palestinians, who at least prior to 1988, constituted a clear majority. However, in Al-Az'ar's (1995) view, "this integration was symbolic, since the centers of power remained in the hands of original Jordanians. Thus granting the refugees citizenship rights did not stop their close monitoring and suspicion of their intentions" (p. 14).

When the 1954 Jordanian Nationality Law went into effect, Palestinians on both sides of the Jordan River were given Jordanian citizenship. This remained the case until 1988, when Jordan removed its legal claim to the West Bank. Although West Bankers ceased to be Jordanian citizens, they continued to hold Jordanian passports valid for five years.

Palestinians who fled during the 1967 war from the West Bank to Jordan, whether as first-time refugees (the so-called "displaced") or second-time refugees from the 1948 war, are considered Jordanian citizens. Palestinians from Gaza who fled to Jordan after the 1967 war, most of whom are refugees for the second time, do not enjoy the same rights as other Palestinians in Jordan; latecomers also are not considered Jordanian citizens. Gazans who were expelled by Kuwait after the Gulf

War and ended up in Jordan constitute the most disadvantaged group of all. They are not entitled to hold Jordanian citizenship or own property, and technically they are not allowed to work.

Although the latest Jordanian census of 1995 yielded estimates of the size of the Palestinian population in Jordan, the government has refused to make the figures public for fear of contributing to national divisions (Reuters World Report 1996). As shown in chapter 1, UNRWA estimates the number of Palestinian refugees in Jordan at 1,240,000. This number does not include those displaced in 1967 or the refugees who did not appear on UNRWA's original roster.

Lebanon

Lebanon is unique among Arab countries for its stringent policies toward the Palestinian refugees on several fronts and has different classifications of the more than 350,000 refugees within its territory. First are the 1948 refugees, who are registered with UNRWA and with the Department of General Security and Refugee Affairs and who are technically given special travel documents. Second are refugees who arrived in Lebanon from second or third countries, who are not considered legal residents of the country and are denied government services. This category includes those not registered with UNRWA, even though they may benefit from UNRWA's services. The third category covers the 1967 refugees who are not registered with UNRWA and who are technically illegal in the country (Al-Az'ar 1995; Takkenberg 1995).

It is important to bear in mind that, between 1948 and 1951, the Lebanese government did offer the refugees material and moral support. In subsequent years, however, the treatment of the Palestinians deteriorated substantially. Natur (1993) described current official Lebanese policy objectives toward the Palestinians as

- reducing their numbers by means of emigration;

- redistributing them to other Arab countries;

- severing the links between the various Palestinian refugee camps in Lebanon;

- denying them civil rights, including the right to work; and

• refusing to establish a legal and administrative official framework, with accountability and transparency, which would define in clear terms the status of Palestinian refugees.

Since the start of the Middle East peace talks in 1991, Lebanon has progressively and severely restricted Palestinian movement within and into the country, even for those who are registered with UNRWA and carry valid travel documents. Palestinians in Lebanon are denied access to public education. Those who are registered with UNRWA receive free education until the end of grade nine; after that, they have to pay for schooling, not easy for a community with a high unemployment rate. By law, working in the public sector requires proof of citizenship for at least ten years, and in the private sector, Palestinian job seekers need a special permit. As a result, Palestinians work in the informal economy, are exploited through low wages, and are not covered by existing unemployment and welfare legislation.

Lebanese law also prohibits Palestinians from working in professional fields such as law, medicine, and engineering, even though these occupations are open to professionals from other countries as long as Lebanese counterparts are treated in a reciprocal manner by the same countries. Although the government has withheld Lebanese nationality from the overwhelming majority of Palestinian refugees, in the early 1950s it did grant nationality to an estimated 50,000 Christian Palestinians and to a much smaller number of affluent Sunni Palestinians. Thus, the majority of the close to 350,000 Palestinians in Lebanon registered with UNRWA remain stateless (Natur 1993).

Syria

The more than 300,000 Palestinians in Syria are closely monitored through the General Authority for Palestinian Refugees, a department within the Ministry of Social and Labor Affairs. The Palestinians in Syria enjoy a large measure of economic and social integration but lack corresponding political rights. They have equal access to government-provided social services, education, and employment opportunities, including civil service jobs. However, in line with Syria's nationalist rhetoric on the right of return, Palestinians in Syria are not allowed to own arable land or more than one house, nor can they participate in politics.

Egypt

There are no publicly available accurate estimates of the Palestinians in Egypt; researchers note that the figure could vary from 70,000 to 100,000 (Raei 1995). Egypt's policy toward its Palestinians has gone through three phases. Immediately after the 1948 exodus, Egypt decided to settle Palestinian refugees in urban centers and not camps, reject international relief efforts, close the gates to further immigration, and have state agencies monitor the Palestinians closely. During this phase, Palestinians were offered limited opportunities to work, accompanied by some financial assistance. In the second phase, from the mid-1950s until the mid-1970s (known as the Golden Era), Palestinians were granted rights equal to those of Egyptians, while retaining their Palestinian identity. During the third phase, which began in the mid-1970s and continues to the present time, the Egyptian government has rescinded many of these rights in the civil, economic, and social fields and has treated Palestinians as foreigners.

Initially, Egypt recognized the travel rights of those Palestinians who held passports issued by the British Mandatory government of Palestine. Now, most Palestinians are issued temporary (from one to three years) Egyptian travel documents whose renewal has become extremely difficult. The situation of Gazan refugees who left to work in the Gulf, and whose Egyptian-issued permits expired, fall under this category. Palestinians without valid travel documents cannot obtain work permits in Egypt. In terms of social services and education, Palestinians are now treated as foreigners who have to pay for any public services received (Takkenberg 1995; Raei 1995).

Gulf Countries

The decline in the relatively good fortunes of Palestinian refugees in the Gulf started in 1980, a decade before the Gulf War. In the early 1970s, between 80 and 90 percent rated their conditions in the Gulf states as good; by 1980, that percentage had already dropped to between 65 and 75 percent. Nour's interviews (1993) with Palestinian returnees demonstrates clearly the impact of the Gulf War on the treatment accorded to the Palestinians. Government policies, employment opportunities, public reaction, and dealings with employers deteriorated significantly.

The number of Palestinians in the Gulf states dwindled drastically after their expulsion from Kuwait in 1991. Originally, it was estimated that around 30,000 Palestinians remained in Kuwait. A few have gone back (with Jordanian passports), and the overall figure now is between 50,000 and 70,000 Palestinians in Kuwait, who are closely monitored by the authorities. They are still subject to the same, if not more restrictive, laws that Kuwait instituted prior to the expulsion. It is next to impossible for foreign-born nationals and their offspring, even if locally born, to obtain Kuwaiti citizenship either by birth or by naturalization. Similarly, non-Kuwaitis do not have the right to own their homes or businesses. Owning a business is possible only if there is a Kuwaiti partner (or *kafiel*, i.e., guarantor) and the majority ownership is registered in a Kuwaiti name. Employees who reach the age of retirement must leave the country. Educational opportunities in government-funded schools are very limited to Palestinians at all levels. The same regulations that govern Palestinians in Kuwait apply to Palestinians in Saudi Arabia and other Gulf countries.

Iraq

Although the original influx of the 1948 Palestinians into Iraq was no more than 5,000 refugees, it is estimated that Iraq now has close to 50,000 Palestinians. These include some of the Palestinians who were expelled from Kuwait during the Gulf War. Iraq grants citizenship to all Arabs who apply for it, including Palestinians. Palestinians in Iraq enjoy the same rights as Iraqi citizens except for the right to vote.

Libya

Until fairly recently, tens of thousands of Palestinians in Libya were allowed to leave and enter the country freely. The majority of the Palestinians in Libya are professionals and skilled workers. Claiming the right-of-return to Palestine as justification, Libyan legislation (similar to that in other Arab countries) does not allow Palestinians to own immovable property. Their situation deteriorated significantly during 1995, when Libya expelled a sizable segment of its Palestinian community. One group of those expelled attempted to travel to Lebanon and then to Syria. After being refused outright by the former, Palestinians with Syrian documents were granted permission to enter Syria. With the right of entry into other Arab countries and the West Bank and Gaza severely restricted by Arab governments and by Israel, most of the Palestinian expellees now live in refugee camps along the Libyan-Egyptian border.

The Maghreb

As mentioned above, the Maghreb countries (Morocco, Tunisia, and Algeria), along with Egypt, are signatories to the 1951 UN Convention on the Status of Refugees. The number of Palestinians residing in the Maghreb countries has always been small, and they have not suffered from the blatant discrimination exercised by other Arab governments. Agreements between the PLO and the North African governments regulate the presence of Palestinians in these countries. Permits for exit and entry are coordinated between the PLO offices and the relevant authorities of the host countries.

Social and Living Conditions

Lebanon

As will be evident throughout this study, the situation of the Palestinians in Lebanon is worse than that of any other Palestinian refugee community. This is confirmed in a thorough study carried out by Suhail Natur (1993), a Palestinian lawyer who lives in Lebanon. Basing his estimates on the original figure of 100,000 Palestinian refugees who settled in Lebanon in 1948 and applying a 3 percent rate of natural increase, he calculated the minimum number of Palestinian refugees in 1993 to be 378,135. The Lebanese government, on the other hand, tends to (over)estimate the size of the Palestinian population at around 500,000, in order to show that it is shouldering a large responsibility. UNRWA puts the figure at 340,000.

It is estimated by Natur (1993) that between 30,000 and 40,000 Palestinians died in Lebanon's various internal wars and in the wars between Israel and the Palestinians. As a result of the Lebanese civil war and the various Israeli incursions into Lebanon, most notably the 1982 invasion, which resulted in the massacre of Palestinian refugees in Sabra and Shatila camps, internal migration has been estimated at between 6,000 and 8,000 families (roughly between 31,000 and 43,000 individuals). This internal migration has taken its toll on a population that was already suffering from a harsh refugee experience.

In the sphere of education, Natur pointed out that repeated internal displacements have contributed to long absences from schools by children, and poverty prevented their families from paying for private education. Children who were able to find schools in which to enroll moved to new homes that lacked electricity and in most cases consisted of one room housing an average of seven individuals--an environment hardly conducive to learning. Due to repeated displacements and movement from one school to another, "transient students" became a familiar feature of Palestinian family life. It is thus not surprising that the condition of internal refugees on the move has resulted in adverse psychological and social consequences.

Natur described the social structure of the camps where extended families were transplanted mainly from rural Palestine to urban camp life in Lebanon. Dispersal notwithstanding, political identifications were determined by traditional familial and even tribal connections, which were maintained in the camps. The situation changed with the extension of PLO authority to the camps, in particular as a result of the 1969 Cairo agreement which gave the Palestinians autonomy in running their own affairs. However, with the weakening of the PLO presence in the camps after the Israeli invasion of 1982, Natur claimed, there occurred a restrengthening of the role of old family ties in local Palestinian politics.

Natur described life in the camps in the shadow of UNRWA as having both positive and negative facets. Although UNRWA provided much-needed financial and economic assistance, it also contributed to the emergence of a feeling of dependency among the camp population. Because of differences in economic circumstances, conflicts arose between camp residents and Palestinian refugees who lived outside the camps. The Palestinians themselves did not attempt to improve their living conditions in the camps, because they viewed the camps as temporary places of residence. Camp-dwelling Palestinians in particular did not mix with Lebanese society: Not only did the latter reject them, but they, in turn, were wary of resettlement attempts in Lebanon.

Using 1989 as a reference point, Natur claimed that the dependency ratio (proportion of the population below 15 and above 60 years of age to the rest) among the Palestinians stood at 772/1,000--a very high ratio. Some 40 percent of the population was below age fifteen. Not more than 5.1 percent of Palestinian women in Lebanon participate in the labor market.

Natur observed that, since 1962, Palestinians have been treated as foreigners or worse in matters related to employment. Substantially more work permits were issued to foreigners than to Palestinians. Only 1,300 remain employed in PLO institutions in Lebanon, and they receive low wages compared to the rest of the country. For example, a PLO-employed doctor receives a monthly salary of $97 and a street cleaner $33 per month, whereas a teacher working for UNRWA receives $365 per month. Social assistance given by the PLO to needy Palestinians who lost family members in the various wars ranges from $23 a month for an unmarried person to $35 for a married one; in 1982, by contrast, PLO assistance levels stood at $100 and $125, respectively.

The situation of the Palestinians in the 1990s is not only worse than any other Palestinian community elsewhere, but also the worst of any other group in Lebanon. The author attributed this to five factors: a continued population increase among the Palestinians that is unaccompanied by new openings in the labor market; the almost total disappearance of Palestinian job-creation prospects after the eclipse of the PLO in 1982; the entry of Lebanese of working age into the labor market in large numbers following the dissolution of the Lebanese militias, shrinking the job prospects for Palestinians even further; the return of additional Palestinians to Lebanon as a consequence of the Gulf War, adding to the ranks of the unemployed; and the near-total collapse of the Lebanese currency which contributed to high inflation in the country (this last factor affecting the position of the community in Lebanon compared to Palestinians elsewhere). Thus in 1992, the unemployment rate among the Palestinians in Lebanon was put at 38 percent. According to UNRWA, 11 percent of its registered refugees qualified as hardship cases, the highest in any of UNRWA's areas of operation.

The Lebanese government's recent reconstruction plans have side-stepped the problems faced by Palestinian refugees, particularly the internally displaced among them. Natur pointed out that the plans to rebuild shattered Beirut are bound to contribute to further displacement of the already dispossessed Palestinian community. Whereas the government duly compensates displaced Lebanese with land, housing, and financial assistance, no such plans are in place for Palestinian refugees who will be displaced by rebuilding projects. On the contrary, the government forces them to choose between low compensation or eviction from the camps and shantytowns surrounding Beirut.

Direct and indirect contributions of the Palestinians to the Lebanese economy have not been insignificant. Natur estimated that the Palestinian refugees who went to Lebanon brought with them capital valued at £3.7

million. UNRWA contributes close to $30 million to the Lebanese economy annually. UNRWA continues to offer the only tangible assistance to Palestinians in Lebanon (and elsewhere), but reductions in its budget and mismanagement and corruption within UNRWA itself have further contributed to a deterioration in the Palestinians' living conditions. These observations are corroborated by Rosemary Sayigh (1995).

Housing for Palestinian refugees in Lebanon is probably worse than that in any other Palestinian refugee community. Natur estimated housing density in the 1990s to be four-to-five persons per room, with the average area of a dwelling at 80 square meters. Sixty percent live in rent-free housing provided by UNRWA, 30 percent pay rent, and the rest own their dwellings. Although property ownership is not allowed by Palestinians, a few have managed to become quite wealthy.

How do the Lebanese react to the Palestinian presence in their midst? In a representative sample of close to 1,000 Lebanese reflecting the main religious groupings in the country, Khashan (1995) concluded that "despite the unpopularity of resettlement, more respondents were willing to accept resettlement than those who were against it. This is probably the case because many Lebanese felt they have little control over events in their country" (p. 12). A closer look at the data, however, reveals a more complicated picture of generalized hostility toward the refugees that transcends confessional lines. For example, 75 percent rejected the resettlement of Palestinians in Lebanon, a figure that was fairly consistent across the country's various religious denominations. Only one-third referred to friendship with Palestinians. One-third thought that resettlement of the refugees would be imposed upon Lebanon, and three-quarters rated the consequences of such resettlement as damaging to the country, leading to the resumption of the civil war, further economic crises, demographic imbalance, and the creation of an additional "sectarian" group.

The harsh attitude of the Lebanese government toward the Palestinians was the subject of a memorandum presented by various Palestinian groups at a meeting with Lebanese prime minister Rafik Al-Hariri in February 1994 (Memorandum of Meeting 1994). The memorandum assured the Lebanese government that the Palestinians would abide by the PLO Charter and its insistence on returning to Palestine and that they had no desire to remain in Lebanon. Among the problems that the Palestinians face in Lebanon, the memorandum noted the following:

• a decrease in UNRWA budget allocations;

• the presence of close to 15,000 families whose breadwinners had died in the various wars and upheavals and who were not receiving any financial assistance from the PLO;

• close to 6,000 families displaced during the fighting, whose homes had been destroyed and who were not allowed to return and rebuild their shelters;

• endemic discrimination in employment; and

• shortage of housing in the camps.

Among their demands, the Palestinians asked the Lebanese government to

• allow Palestinians to rebuild their homes in the camps;

• ease restrictions on employment and allow professionals to practice their specialties;

• allow displaced people to return to their previous places of residence;

• end the practice of treating the Palestinians on a par with other foreigners in Lebanon; and

• establish a tripartite committee comprised of the UNRWA, the Palestinians, and the Lebanese government to resolve outstanding differences.

Most of these demands were turned down by the prime minister. He claimed that granting the Palestinians civil rights might be construed as a sign that Lebanon had agreed to their resettlement. Economically, Lebanon was unable to absorb Palestinian professionals at a time when Lebanese with similar qualifications were unable to find jobs. Hariri promised to look into the situation of the internally displaced people but insisted that any return of the displaced must be to Sunni areas near

Sidon and that none should be allowed to return to Beirut. In light of this response, and Hariri's publicly declared position that Lebanon would be pressuring the Palestinians to leave the country, the future does not look bright for the Palestinians in Lebanon.

A moderate solution for the Palestinian refugee predicament in Lebanon was offered by Salam (1993), a Lebanese lawyer. Salam proposed granting certain specific civil and social rights to the Palestinians in Lebanon, who would simultaneously be granted citizenship by a future Palestinian state in the West Bank and Gaza. Under this proposal, Palestinians would not be allowed to vote, run for political office, hold public sector jobs, or invest in sectors of the economy having direct bearing on national security; they could work and have freedom of movement, as long as reciprocal rights would be enjoyed by Lebanese nationals in areas under Palestinian jurisdiction.

Syria

Of the main four regions with refugee concentrations (the occupied territories, Jordan, Lebanon, and Syria), Syria has received the least attention from researchers. In a doctoral thesis on the demography of the Palestinians in Syria, Maswada (1994) discovered that on some indicators, such as literacy and university attainment, Palestinian rates in Syria surpassed those of Palestinians elsewhere. Between 1960 and 1992, illiteracy declined from 29 to 6 percent for males and from 66 to 19 percent for females. Similarly, Palestinian university graduates accounted for 4 percent of the Palestinian population in Syria in 1992, up from 0.5 percent in 1960. According to the author, these are higher than the rates for Syrian nationals and for Palestinians in Lebanon and the occupied territories. Rates of participation in the labor force increased from 33 percent in 1960 to 46 percent in 1992. This overall depressed rate of labor participation is due mainly to the lower rates for women, which stood at 13 percent in 1992.

Bearing in mind that Palestinian refugees in Syria came mainly from rural backgrounds in Palestine, current data show a remarkable urban transformation in terms of values, occupational specialization, and places of residence. In comparing the Palestinians to native Syrians, Maswada found that the Palestinians have placed greater emphasis on education, experienced a sharp rise in entry to the labor force, raised the mean age of first marriage, and reduced fertility and mortality rates. This, in the author's view, supports the thesis that the Palestinian community in Syria has "unique demographic and socioeconomic characteristics" and disproves the "cradle revenge" thesis, according to which Palestinians would be expected to have a high fertility rate as a political act to enhance the chances of their national survival (Maswada 1994, 62).

Although their living conditions in Syria are substantially better than in other countries, Palestinians manifest social characteristics associated with refugee communities in general. In a study of "social marginality" among 150 cleaning workers (96 men and 54 women) drawn from Syria's refugee camps, Naser 'Atiyyeh (1993) noted that the morphology of the camps reflects in large measure the experience of the refugees in Palestine. For example, those who came from urban centers in Palestine, such as Tiberias and Safad, settled near urban locations such as Damascus or Aleppo and sought work in those cities. Those who came from rural areas in Palestine settled in camps that are in close proximity to agricultural work and farming. Like other refugee communities, the camps remained self-contained settlements, with their own internal social structure and stratification system. Here too the refugees provided unskilled labor to the surrounding service and construction sectors.

This is not, however, a deprived community. Seventy percent of Palestinians in Syria own their homes, 18 percent live with their extended families, and the remaining 12 percent rent their homes. Even manual laborers do well through supplementing their regular wages with work in the informal sector. Thus, the average salary of a worker in a sample of marginal workers was around 5,600 Syrian pounds, compared with an engineer who made only 3,000 Syrian pounds a month ('Attiyeh 1993).

However, some of the laborers in 'Attiyeh's case study were not organized, had no written contracts with their employers, and did not even own the tools with which they worked. In other words, they were easily replaceable and at the mercy of their bosses. The marginal nature of the work had its health cost. More than half of the workers in the sample complained of old-age illnesses, such as spinal injuries, chest pain, breathing difficulties, and stomach problems. This is significant because more than one-third of the sample was between fifteen and thirty years of age.

In deciding on family size, the majority seemed to be guided by economic and personal considerations. Fifty-eight percent favored the use of birth control, and 40 percent were against it. Those favoring birth control cited economic and familial reasons. For the latter, preference for large families was dictated by religious convictions and tradition. This lends further support for rejecting the "cradle revenge" thesis.

A more comprehensive study of the Palestinians in Syria was carried out by Chafic Kamal (1994), who underscored the economic and social heterogeneity of the refugee camps. For example, the Yarmouk camp near Damascus registers a per capita income of 635 Syrian pounds, nearly twice that recorded for Dara'a camp in the south and Jaramana camp near Damascus. Between the two extremes lie the camps of Homs and Hama. Overall, however, the author estimated that the income of Palestinians in Syria is below that of Syrian citizens.

The inability of Palestinians to move freely across international borders, including to other Arab states, limits the activity of the entrepreneurs among them. Kamal discovered that there is little trust in the peace process among this strata of Palestinians, and most are unwilling to take risks and make investments in the absence of any international guarantees and lack of political stability in the occupied territories.

These findings are confirmed in another study of Palestinian entrepreneurs in Syria. Sari Hanafi (1995) argued that the Palestinians in Syria are too integrated to want to leave to a new Palestinian state and too old to start new ventures and are deterred by the precarious situation in the occupied territories.

Egypt

In a qualitative case study of twenty Palestinians living in Cairo (two male and eighteen female refugees from the 1948 and 1967 wars), Raei (1995) set out to ascertain the degree to which their experiences resembled that of refugees elsewhere. Excluding two officials (one PLO and the other UNRWA), four of the eighteen in the sample had been uprooted once and the rest between two and four times. Although the 1948 refugees came from urban backgrounds and were better off to begin with, compared to the 1967 refugees who came from Gaza and who were of peasant background, their overall experiences were similar. The author concluded that all Palestinian refugees "suffer from similar problems, such as financial difficulties, family disintegration, inability to pursue better education or jobs and the threat of residence [permit] cancellation" (Raei 1995, 40).

Several of Raei's findings suggest a commonality of experiences with other Palestinian refugee communities. First, the PLO ceased to offer the

Palestinians any real aid after the 1991 Gulf War. As a result, attitudes toward the PLO were basically negative. Second, very few of those interviewed expressed the wish or considered it practical to return to Palestine. Third, the level of educational attainment of Palestinians living in Egypt, particularly of girls, had noticeably deteriorated. Fourth, there was a growing conservative sentiment about the role of women in society and a strengthening of the belief that women belong in the home. Finally, immediate rectification of the Palestinians' economic, political, and human rights conditions was possible only by granting them international protection through legal recognition of their status as refugees, possibly through measures similar to those used by refugees who fell under the jurisdiction of the UNHRC.

West Bank and Gaza

One of the first comprehensive attempts to assess the living conditions of the Palestinians in the West Bank and Gaza was carried out in 1992 by Norway's Institute for Applied Social Science, in collaboration with Palestinian researchers (Heiberg et al. 1992). The study tapped a nationally representative sample of 2,500 heads of households and respondents above fifteen years of age from the West Bank, Gaza, and Arab Jerusalem.

The study's focus was on the concept of "living conditions." An individual's welfare "is defined not so much by the economic goods he or she possesses, but by the ability of the individual to exercise choice and to affect the course of his or her own life" (p. 13). The study had clear policy implications in mind, primarily "to assist Palestinians in planning and measuring the course of their own social and economic development" (p. 16).

The study found that slightly less than one-half of the population of the West Bank is below the age of fourteen; in Gaza, it is 51 percent. Contrary to expectations, refugee households have fewer members than nonrefugee households, possibly due to emigration in search of employment and education in neighboring Arab countries. Official Israeli data from the early 1990s place the infant mortality rate in the West Bank and Gaza at 25 per 1,000. Palestinian researchers' put it at more than 70 per 1,000; the Norwegian-sponsored study put it at 50 deaths per 1,000 live births for infants under one year of age.

The Norwegian study also found that significant transformation is taking place in family structure. For example, the nuclear family is gradually becoming more prevalent than the traditional extended family and the *hamula* (clan). Still, bearing in mind that three or more persons per room constitutes overcrowdedness by international standards, the figures for the entire territories show that about 28 percent live three persons or more per room, with overcrowdedness reaching around 40 percent in Gaza and 20 percent in Arab Jerusalem.

The study's assessment of infrastructural services is based on the extent of availability of potable and piped water, electricity, telephones, and sewage. According to the survey, 70 percent of the people live in homes with "average" amenities; 18 percent have "poor" infrastructural services, and the remaining 12 percent enjoy "above average" conditions. Contrary to expectations, the poorest localities are refugee camps in the West Bank, and not the Gaza Strip, where between 75 percent and 85 percent of the households are rated as having "average" infrastructural amenities. However, as admitted by the authors, this assessment does not take into account the absence of "vital municipal services, such as sanitation, rubbish disposal and roads" (Heiberg et al. 1992, 88). Nor did it take into account that in the rural West Bank only 50 percent of the households (at most) have electricity on a regular basis, and that in the West Bank as a whole only two-thirds of the homes have electricity on a twenty-four-hour basis. Likewise, the study did not take the quality of water into account; the authors recognized that Gaza's water is known for its poor quality. Yet, the study bravely stated that "infrastructural services are very good in relation to developing countries in general" (p. 88).

Rural and West Bank refugee camps reported significantly higher rates of acute illness and injuries than other localities in the survey. Camp residents in the West Bank showed the highest level of psychological distress, followed by Arab Jerusalem and West Bank villages and towns. Gaza scored lower on the distress index than Arab Jerusalem and the West Bank, raising an interesting anomaly:

[L]iving conditions in Gaza are generally worse than in the West Bank. So why do Gazans report fewer symptoms of distress? One possible explanation may indeed be that people in Gaza have a clear sense of collective meaning and common purpose. A greater sense of cohesiveness, originating in a more traditional family structure, may also contribute as a protective factor. . . . Then again, the explanation could well be that Gaza residents are less prone to recognizing and

> expressing symptoms of psychological distress. (p. 124)

Perception of social conflict is highest among Jerusalemites, whose living conditions are better than the other regions and is correlated with high distress level. It is interesting to note that communal life in Gaza has produced an "us-and-them" view of the world, where internal conflict based on class, age, and gender is less significant than it is in other places.

Refugees who finished UNRWA schools have a higher educational attainment level than nonrefugees. Likewise, UNRWA-educated children have higher literacy rates than those attending (Israeli) government-run schools, but among those fifteen to nineteen years old, women do better than men in terms of literacy. More girls than boys drop out of school by the time they reach grade nine. Females in the West Bank show the highest illiteracy rates, reaching one-third of the total sample of women. However, when the figures are broken down by age and gender, women between the ages of fifteen and nineteen years exhibit the lowest illiteracy rate in the entire sample. Furthermore, in the next age group, twenty to twenty-nine years, women are not far behind men in literacy. High illiteracy rates are mainly prevalent among women forty years and older.

Patriarchy appears to pose the biggest impediment to women's advancement in Palestinian society. Households headed by women, which comprise 10 percent of all households in the sample, are economically worse off than any other group in the survey. Compared to men, the position of women inside and outside refugee camps is a disadvantaged one, whether in the economic, political, or educational spheres. The patriarchal nature of Palestinian society is confirmed by the Norwegian study, which noted that

> men have more influence than women (in the family, society, and neighborhood), the middle aged more than the very old or the young. In short, in Palestinian society education seems to have done little to erode ascribed status as the determinant of authority. (Heiberg et al. 1992, 147)

Although increased education for both men and women is positively correlated with the belief in women's right to work outside the home, the fact remains that 57 percent of the men do not think it is acceptable for women to work outside the home, 80 percent of the men in the sample believe that Western dress is inappropriate for Palestinian women, and men are evenly split between those who favor women making their own decisions regarding marriage and those who prefer family-arranged marriages. The study noted that "one conclusion that might be drawn from this data could be that measures to effect improvements in the status of women and attitudes toward them should be chiefly directed toward men" (p. 156).

The intifada appears to have given rise to two contradictory forces of social change with clear consequences for Palestinian society in general and for women and the young in particular. On the one hand, active participation by young people in daily confrontations with the Israeli army which resulted in large numbers of them being injured, detained, killed, and traumatized appears, at the normative level, to have ruptured the traditional authority structure in the family and community. As the authority of the elders appeared to wane, anti-authority attitudes by the young spread to the schools and to society at large. Teachers, parents, and older people became powerless in the face of a militant young generation.

On the other hand, Palestinian society, which had prided itself in recent times on its relatively secular tradition, seems to have awakened an opposing current, that of conservative Islamic values. As the primary carrier of this banner, the Hamas movement has called for a holy war against Israeli occupation and for Palestinian women to abandon Western mores, denounced mixed education, and emphasized religious teachings in the curriculum. Thus, patriarchy was further reinforced by stressing the home as the proper place for women, with education and work outside the home relegated to a secondary status (United Nations Development Program [UNDP] 1995; Al-Maliki 1994).

The Norwegian study found that camp dwellers are the worst off economically, followed by refugees outside the camps. Geographically, the wealthiest regions are Arab Jerusalem and the central subdistricts of the West Bank. The study, which was based on self-reporting, pointed out that the most deprived groups were the ones who suffered most as a result of the Gulf War and the decline in remittances. According to the study, employment was least stable in Gaza and most stable in Arab Jerusalem, with the West Bank falling somewhere in between. Close to 80 percent of the workers held one job during the year previous to the survey, but they had worked, on average, four weeks or less in the previous two months, a pattern that bespeaks their shaky employment profile. Participation rates in the labor force among men, which reach around 80 percent, conceal the fact that only 42 percent hold full-time jobs and 48 percent part-time jobs. Among Gazan men, the participation rate for full-time employment is a mere 25 percent. Participation rates for women hover around 15 percent.

In response to the question "for whom would you be willing to make the ultimate sacrifice?", the family was ranked first. This was followed by the "Palestinian people," the "Islamic nation," and (last) the "Arab nation." However, attachment to the family is weak among the young, compared to the middle-aged. Close to 45 percent of the women in the youngest age bracket directed their loyalty toward the Palestinian people, compared to one-third who mentioned the family as the prime focus of their loyalty.

There is no doubt that the Norwegian survey provides an important baseline for future research on the Palestinians in general and those in the occupied territories in particular. Yet, there are various reasons (beyond the scope of the present survey) why its chapter on stratification is unable to give a useful definition of poverty against which the well-being of the population surveyed can be reliably and realistically assessed. This, I believe, is the most serious shortcoming of the study.

As a possible filler of this lacuna in the Norwegian study, a report on poverty was recently prepared by the Palestine Economic Policy Research Institute in Jerusalem (Sha'ban and Al-Botmeh 1995). Through the use of data provided by private service organizations dedicated to helping the poor, information from UNRWA regarding its hardship cases, and the Palestinian Ministry of Social Affairs, the authors of this study reached a "lower-bound" poverty estimate (based on $500 per capita annually) of 20 percent for Gaza and 10 percent for the West Bank, with a combined proportion of 14 percent of the population in the territories living below the poverty line.

Other research shows that unemployment and poverty are more pervasive among Palestinian refugees than the Norwegian and the above-cited Palestinian studies seem to indicate. In a study of a small refugee camp in the West Bank, Hazboun (1992) drew a more realistic picture. His survey, carried out in 1990, covered 149 of a total of 155 households in the camp, whose population of around 1,000 inhabitants was originally uprooted from Beit-Jibrin village inside Israel. In this camp, the average family size exceeded six, and the level of educational attainment was quite low. Twenty-one percent of those between twenty-five and sixty-four years of age (i.e., those usually considered to be of working age) were unemployed. If the fifteen- to twenty-five-year-olds are added to the pool of the unemployed, the rate rises to 40 percent. Of the unemployed among the twenty-five to sixty-four-year-olds, close to 80 percent had been unemployed for more than twelve months prior to the survey. Even though these workers paid income taxes during their working lives, they did not benefit from any social security program or retirement pensions.

The average income per household in the camp was estimated to be New Israeli Shekels (NIS) 835 (around $300) at the beginning of 1990; it dropped to NIS 736 three years later. When UNRWA assistance (which is provided to 148 households classified as hardship cases), savings, and other means of assistance from relatives were taken into account, household income rose to NIS 1,424. However, because the average size of the Palestinian family is six, this total household income remains significantly below the Israeli poverty line, which is defined as NIS 1,700 per month for a four-person family.

Thus, as the Palestinian Authority (PA) assumed partial control of the occupied territories in accordance with the terms of the Oslo accords, unemployment in the West Bank and Gaza hovered around 40 percent, according to UNRWA estimates (UNRWA 1992c), with the per-capita gross domestic product (GDP) amounting to $2,175 in the West Bank and $1,131 in Gaza, compared to $11,878 in Israel (Fischer, Rodrik, and Tuma 1994; Zureik 1994).

The Norwegian study cited above was the first full-scale research carried out by one of the so-called shepherds within the RWG. Since its publication, several other policy-oriented studies of Palestinian communities have been conducted. For example, the EU (1994) commissioned a comprehensive study of assistance programs to the refugees in UNRWA's six fields of operation: relief and social services, physical infrastructure, health, education, vocational training, and income generation. The EU study concluded the following: (1) there was a lack of coordination between the providers of assistance and the various sectors, leading to duplication of services in some sectors and absence of services in others; (2) there was insufficient flexibility in the assistance provided; because of the diversity of refugee situations and needs, programs that were centrally administered were often incapable of meeting the needs of their clients; (3) an effective monitoring mechanism to insure accountability in aid distribution was lacking; (4) aid given should not differentiate between refugees and nonrefugees living in the surrounding host societies; this recommendation was based on the finding that, on several indicators, refugees were hardly distinguishable from (and in some cases better off than) those in the surrounding communities. The stipulation was added that the administration of aid should not "prejudice their [refugee] right or preempt final status negotiations" (EU 1994, Executive Summary, 3).

Salim Tamari (1994) objected to the latter recommendation and discounted the claim of nonprejudice in the final status phase, as follows:

> To claim that such aid shall not prejudice the future status of refugees is not very accurate since refugees with improved social and economic status are likely to move out of the camps, to migrate to other countries, and in general to relegate their refugee condition to an abstract political commitment. Thus those who remain in the camps inside Palestine tend to be the urban poor, and consequently the status of camps has increasingly acquired the form and "normal" urban slums in recent years.

The EU's statement about nonprejudicing refugee rights, Tamari warned, "will become a formula for covering up schemes for relocation and resettlement of refugees, without satisfying their needs and aspirations," unless this is accompanied by concrete protections ensured during future negotiations on the refugee issue (Tamari 1994, 2-3).

Two of the recommendations reached by the EU-sponsored study are very similar to the suggestions long advocated by Israeli anthropologist Emmanuel Marx. In an overview of his previous work on Palestinian refugees in the occupied territories, Marx blamed UNRWA and, surprisingly, the Israeli government for extending the life of refugee camps. UNRWA, he claimed, has acted

> like many other bureaucracies, altered its targets, grown in size and become a self-sustaining organization. This will go some way towards explaining why the number of refugees has grown over the years and why so many people still live in "refugee camps" (1992, 281).

On the other hand, instead of integrating the refugees into neighboring communities to "which the camps have become similar," the Israeli government has kept them segregated, as happened in the Gaza housing experiment. By allowing some 8,500 households to live in new housing units and apart from the surrounding community, the Israel government "gave [an] impetus for the refugees to revive their refugee identity" (p. 293).

The EU recommendations also converge with those outlined in a six-volume study by the World Bank (1994). In *Human Resources and Social Policy*, the World Bank study, which focuses on health, education, and social services, concluded that deficiencies in human resources are rooted in poor "governance" (i.e., lack of accountability, rational management, and reliable information) rather than in scarcity of resources. What emerges clearly from the World Bank's study is an approach that seeks to explain the problems of development mainly in terms of local conditions--political, bureaucratic, and informational. Although local conditions and style of governance undoubtedly play an important role in the management of human resources, it is imperative to examine on an equal footing the role of structural factors which, in the case of the West Bank and Gaza, are rooted in a dependent relationship forged over the years between the occupying power and the occupied territories.

The report of the International Labour Organization (ILO 1994) and Palestinian planners (Jerusalem Media and Communications Center [JMCC] 1994) provide a useful antidote to the thrust of the approaches of the World Bank and the EU. For the ILO, structural factors of the economy are very important to understanding the problems of human resources in the occupied territories. These factors are reflected in a feeble manufacturing sector; an unviable agricultural sector which suffers from shortage of land, water, and access to markets; and an asymmetrical dependence between the occupied territories and Israel in which the former supply the latter with a reservoir of cheap labor and the latter uses the former as a major consuming region for its manufactured goods. The ILO projected that, with 500,000 expected returnees to the occupied territories by the year 2000, the Palestinian employment sector is likely to face a shortage of as many as 90,000 jobs.

The JMCC study elaborated in more detail the consequences of the Israeli occupation for the economy of the territories. It noted, for example, that national planning is handicapped by the absence of reliable and accurate national statistics. Land seizure by Israel has resulted in confiscating close to 65 percent of the West Bank territory and 50 percent of Gaza. And, in contravention of the Hague Regulations and the Fourth Geneva Convention, Israel has implemented a series of military orders which have seriously curtailed Palestinian access to water, land, travel, industrial and agricultural development, and work prospects. In 1992, the report estimates that 13,500 Palestinians were rendered homeless and 3,000 families were living in houses built without permits. Ninety percent of industrial enterprises employ less than ten people, and in Gaza, the average is less than four persons per establishment.

Overall, the JMCC study showed that "de-development" is a more accurate description of the situation in the occupied territories. Whether in agriculture or industry, the occupied territories have experienced a decline in the contribution of these sectors to the overall performance of the economy. The report also noted that the territories were profitable for Israel by generating surplus revenue (over and above Israeli expenditure on the territories) in the late 1980s ($80 million in 1987).

Hisham Awartani (1994) corroborated the negative consequences of Israeli domination of the territories. He noted that 86 percent of all Israeli exports to the territories are industrial, whereas the Palestinian industrial sector contributes a meager 7 percent to GDP. Moreover, Israeli policies have been unduly restrictive in licensing industrial establishments, making credit available to Palestinian entrepreneurs, and in allowing the Palestinians to develop qualified human resources.

To further understand the factors contributing to a stagnant industrial sector in the territories, Awartani cited a study that shows that only 15 percent of workers in large firms and 9 percent in small firms have a high-school education and above, and no more than 6 percent of the labor force in both small- and large-size establishments have some kind of vocational training.

In an analysis of the consequences of "integration" of the territories' economy with that of Israel, in terms of a single currency and Israeli protective commercial policy, Hamed and Sha‘ban (1994) concluded that significant resources have been transferred from the territories to the Israeli treasury. The authors estimated that the Israeli treasury siphoned off between $6 billion and $11 billion in 1990 prices during the period 1970-1987. It is in this context that the authors welcomed the return of expatriate Palestinians, who will bring skills and investments with them and assist in fostering a climate conducive to encouraging foreign investment in general, which may result in breaking the dependent relationship which the territories have with Israel.

Patterns of Adaptation

Accounts of the Palestinian dispersal in 1948 and 1967 are plentiful, but very few studies are available of the adaptation of Palestinian refugees returning to the occupied territories (see the bibliography on Palestinian refugees by Endresen and Zureik 1995). About 30,000 people returned to the West Bank and Gaza after the Gulf War, and an equal number returned along with members of the newly established Palestinian police force in 1994.

A modest start in the direction of understanding patterns of adaptation is provided in several studies reviewed below. An interesting anthropological-ethnographic study of Palestinian refugees in six camps was carried out by the Norwegian Institute for Applied Social Science (Gilen et al. 1994). The camps in question were the Askar camp in the West Bank, near the town of Nablus; the Wihdat and Baqa'a camps in Jordan; and the Rashidiyya camp in south Lebanon. In addition to the four camps, researchers interviewed a limited number of Palestinian refugees who are not camp dwellers but residents of Amman, Jordan. This qualitative research gives readers a feel for the everyday experiences of Palestinians and how they cope under extremely adverse conditions. The focus of the study is on the methods of economic, cultural, political, and residential adaptation and possible integration of Palestinian refugees into the surrounding communities.

Drawing on the work of anthropologists, the authors distinguished between four types of adaptation: assimilation, segregation, incorporation, and migration. Their findings may be summarized under the following seven headings:

(1) Patterns of adaptation were found to correlate with background characteristics (i.e., educated vs. noneducated, town dwellers vs. villagers). For example, well-to-do Palestinian refugees in Jordan found it easier to be assimilated among members of their host community with similar high socioeconomic status compared to refugees with village and peasant backgrounds who felt marginalized.

(2) The process of social construction of communities, the "imagined communities" in Benedict Anderson's sense (1994), was an important feature of camp life. People tended to identify themselves as camp dwellers on the basis of the towns and villages from which they came in

Palestine prior to their exodus. The spatial layout and the camps' neighborhoods usually bore the names of the refugees' places of origin in Palestine.

(3) Unlike refugees in other countries, Palestinians shared with the surrounding host communities a common language, culture, and religion. Yet, these cultural affinities did not lead to successful adaptation because of exclusionary state policies of the host societies.

(4) Compared to camp dwellers, noncamp dwellers tended to engage more in the underground and informal economic sectors. Most camp dwellers belonged to the lower socioeconomic groupings in relation to the host communities.

(5) Partial assimilation, or incorporation, was typical of the Wihdat camp in Jordan and the Askar camp in the West Bank, whereas the Rashidiyya camp in Lebanon was extremely segregated from the neighboring host community.

(6) Skilled and educated Palestinian refugees found it easier to attain citizenship and geographic mobility than other refugees.

(7) Middle-class Palestinians living in Jordan and Lebanon voiced complaints of discrimination in university education, and manual workers complained of discrimination in employment.

Implicitly, Gilen et al. made a case for abolishing the camps, noting that the camps "segregate" their residents from the host societies. This conclusion converges with those reached by the World Bank (1993) and EU (1994) studies discussed above and mirrors the approach adopted in the RWG discussions, which are part of the ongoing multilateral talks of the Madrid peace process. The Norwegian study noted the strong sense of Palestinian identity in the camps, acknowledged the unique contribution of the camps to sustaining that identity, and showed how the camps remain the most salient symbol of Palestinian landlessness and exile. This sense of identity, however, does not prevent camp refugees from feeling abandoned and powerless with regard to their future and right of return.

Two important features are missing from the Norwegian study. First, no strategies or policy implications were drawn to highlight the best ways to help the refugees, indeed the whole of the Palestinian society, achieve economic self-sufficiency so as to be able to absorb returning refugees. There was no discussion of how the issue of return would impinge on the lives of current residents in the occupied territories. Second, the psychosocial consequences of war, displacement, and harassment upon the Palestinians were not examined; nor was there an assessment of possible mechanisms to assist Palestinian families and communities in coping with the stresses and traumas they have undergone.

In another study, Nour (1993) distributed a questionnaire to a sample of 795 returnees to the West Bank and Gaza. Most had spent thirteen years or more in Kuwait, Saudi Arabia, and the Gulf prior to returning to the territories. Seventy-eight percent of the sample gave availability of work as the main reason for going to the Gulf. Slightly more than half preferred to have stayed in the Gulf, their reasons being lack of economic security in the occupied territories and better availability of jobs in the Gulf. Surprisingly, Gazan returnees were found to have a higher level of educational and occupational attainment (67 percent were doctors, engineers, nurses, and teachers) than West Bank returnees (only 32 percent in these categories). This can probably be attributed to Egypt's policy during Nasser's regime, which extended equal treatment to the Palestinians in the public sector and social services.

As expected, Palestinians found employment opportunities severely limited upon their return to the territories. The agriculture, construction, and service sectors provided work for more than 80 percent of West Bank returnees. In Gaza, however, where land is unavailable, 70 percent worked in the service sector alone. Their living conditions on returning home contrasted drastically with those they enjoyed while in Kuwait. Fifty-five percent of West Bank returnees and 81 percent of the returnees to Gaza reported living in places that lacked sewage. When asked to compare the types of consumer goods they had owned in the Gulf and the ones they owned in the occupied territories, 85 percent or more reported that they had owned a washing machine, videocassette recorder, color TV, refrigerator, and private car when in Kuwait; upon returning to the homeland, only 55 percent reported owning a refrigerator, and very few owned a car.

Predictably, the longer the returnee had been abroad, the more difficult the adaptation. In the West Bank, city dwellers were more successful, followed by village dwellers; the least successful were camp residents. In Gaza, regardless of the place of residence, the rate of adaptation was much lower than in the West Bank. Ease of adaptation was also a function of employment and unemployment. The overwhelming majority of those who reported difficult adaptation were unemployed (80-100 percent). Of those who reported movement toward adaptation, between one-half (Gaza) and two-thirds (West Bank) were employed.

A pilot study by the author (Zureik 1996) sheds further light on the fate of Palestinian returnees and their adaptation. The study was based on interviews with forty-two individuals; all except one were spouses who returned under the family reunification scheme. On the whole, both men and women returnees appeared to be qualified in terms of their educational and occupational background. Fifty percent of the men and 66 percent of the women were secondary and postsecondary school graduates. Yet, opportunities to find work commensurate with their qualifications and previous work experience were limited. When work was secured, the income, on the average, was half of what the male returnees had been used to earning abroad.

The economic problems faced by women returnees in the sample were even more serious. Very few of them were employed, at a time when their skills and qualifications were surely needed. Given the low participation rate for women in the labor force in the territories (around 16 percent), special efforts should be made to harness the talents of women, especially those returnees who can contribute to rebuilding their society.

The experience of the returnees under the family reunification program has been mixed. The majority of applicants had to endure a taxing and frustrating process: long waits, uncertainty about the future, and a large number of applications submitted and rejections received. In several cases, applicants had to resort to hiring lawyers at great expense (in some cases running into thousands of dollars). In others, applicants had to turn to human-rights organizations, both Israeli and Palestinian, to assist in understanding and meeting the bureaucratic requirements of the family reunification scheme. In other instances, applicants had to mobilize their connections (*wasta*) with the civil administration, via village *mukhtars* and others, to expedite their applications.

The social and psychological well-being of the returnees, particularly women and children, has been negatively affected when they do not have families in the territories. It is significant that not one of the female returnees in the author's study had either a father or mother living on the West Bank. The role of family ties seems to be equally important in the economic sphere. It appears that in cases where there were family members living in the West Bank, returnees had made special efforts to send remittances and transfer money to build a house for their own future return. None of the survey respondents regarded the West Bank as a place for economic investment ventures, an option included in the questionnaire. This, in all likelihood, is due to perceptions of uncertainty regarding the future.

Patterns of adaptation reveal that, on the whole, returnees adjusted well to their new surroundings. It is possible that long-awaited reunions with families (and in some cases living near the extended family) played a major role in providing social and psychological comfort to them. The majority described their return as a "blessing" and not a "curse." However, the majority of returnees were pessimistic about the political and economic future of the West Bank, but very few considered this a sufficient cause to emigrate. Memories of displacement and multiple uprootings remained fresh in their minds.

A fourth study, carried out by Ahmed and Williams-Ahmed (1993), consisted of interviews with 207 Palestinian and Jordanian returnees to assess the economic impact of the Gulf crisis on Jordan. In terms of educational background, 44 percent had less than high school level, 17 percent were high school graduates, and the rest had either completed their college education or attained some postsecondary education. Whereas close to two-thirds had an annual income of 5,000 Jordanian dinars (JD) while working in Kuwait, only 12 percent maintained this income after their return to Jordan. One of the direct consequences of the Gulf crisis was a decline in remittances. For example, before the crisis, 36 percent indicated that they had sent home between JD 600 and JD 1,000 during the previous year. After the crisis, only 23 percent were able to make such a contribution. Among those who contributed JD 2,000 or more, the proportion declined from 11 percent to slightly less than 4 percent.

Returnees saw their employment prospects for the future as bleak. Fifty-four percent of Ahmed and William-Ahmed's sample indicated that they had been unemployed for more than a year after the war, and 28 percent expected to be unemployed for more than two years. Another 36 percent put their faith in God and fate. Thirty-five percent felt pessimistic about their "economic future," and close to two-thirds felt either uncertain or pessimistic. When asked to indicate a preference for a future place of employment, one-third indicated they would return to the Gulf, 20 percent would go to Palestine, and 15 percent to the U.S. Two-thirds of those who wished to go to Palestine were public sector employees in the Gulf. Of the 26 percent who had worked in professional occupations, only two individuals indicated that they would go to Palestine.

A substantially larger survey of the returnees to Jordan commissioned by the Jordanian government confirmed the overall picture sketched above (National Center for Educational Research and Development [NCERD] 1991). A survey of 100,000 returnees from the Gulf, 80 percent of whom returned from Kuwait, and encompassing more than 16,000 families, showed that as of April 1991, only 20 percent of more than 19,000 previously employed returnees had been able to find jobs. In contrasting previous and present patterns of employment, the survey showed that due to the absence of jobs reflecting the returnees' qualifications, more were now employed in sales and services, and substantially more entered the armed forces (13 percent compared to less than 1 percent previously). One-third of the returnees were subsisting below the poverty line, with an income of less than JD 150 per month per family. When asked to name the problems they faced, the returnees mentioned unemployment (47 percent), finances (21 percent), and finding a place to live (11 percent). A similar picture of the returnees' socioeconomic condition is provided by Lamia Radi (1994).

A topic hardly discussed in the current debate over refugees is the fate of the close to 20 percent of the Palestinians in Israel who were internally displaced in the 1948 war--in other words, those who, while remaining in Israel, have been prevented from returning to their homes and villages. They have organized themselves nationally in an attempt to publicize their plight in the hope that eventually it will be addressed in future talks on final status.

Technically, these internal refugees qualify as refugees under UNRWA's definition of "Palestine refugees," which was discussed in a previous chapter. Moreover, UNRWA did assist these refugees, for a short time, until Israel formally took over the territory and UNRWA's presence in what became Israel was phased out. So far, the Palestinian and Israeli negotiators have not reacted to the plight of the internal refugees. For the Palestinians, the internally displaced are low on their priority list, particularly since their situation is much better than that of the 1948 refugees or those displaced in 1967 in the surrounding host countries. The Israelis can be expected to refuse to discuss the fate of internal refugees on the grounds that they are Israeli citizens with access to Israeli courts.

What are relevant for our purpose are the sociological, not the legal, aspects of this group's uprootedness and their impact on the process of refugee adaptation. Majid Al-Haj (1988, 1986), a Palestinian sociologist from Haifa University, interviewed 133 internal refugees who originally came from rural agricultural areas and currently live in three villages in the Galilee. He uncovered three processes underlying the refugee experience. In the first stage, what he calls the search for asylum (1948-51), displaced people moved in groups encompassing either the same clan or the same village in search of safe places. The second stage, from 1952 to 1957, is characterized by the expectation of return. Like the Palestinian refugees who ended up in neighboring countries, the internal refugees saw their asylum as temporary. During this stage, when the Israeli authorities began confiscating their property and land through the Absentee Property regulations, they became known as the "present absentee" residents of Israel. Loss of property and Israel's military showing in the Suez war of 1956 convinced many that they were unlikely to return to their homes. Still, very few accepted compensation from the government, and most continued to press for their rights to return to their homes (mostly to no avail).

Finally, in the stable settlement stage that began in 1957, where the refugees settled was shaped by the desire to be near Jewish industrial areas in the hope of securing jobs and to reunite fragmented families. Here Al-Haj noted the emergence of a new definition of kinship on the basis not only of biological relatedness but also of village origin. Thus, the politics of space determined friendship and marriage patterns, as well as political loyalties. Whereas Palestinian refugees of the diaspora faced economic and social problems, the internally displaced faced mainly social problems. It was found, for example, that local Palestinians rejected the refugees when it came to marriage, and that "refugees usually did not succeed in penetrating the local primary groups. In most cases, they were isolated, particularly in homogeneous localities, where the refugee-local division formed the main social division" (1988, 162).

Refugee Attitudes and the Peace Process

Refugee public opinion with regard to the peace process and settlement of the Middle East conflict has not been systematically surveyed, but separate, small-scale surveys of refugee communities in various localities, supplemented with qualitative case studies, are available.

A survey of Palestinian refugees in Lebanon, conducted in 1994 among 600 respondents, focused on several issues dealing mainly with the consequences of the peace agreement between Israel and the Palestinians (Sha'ban 1994). The survey revealed that around one-third of the respondents thought that the Jericho-Gaza agreement, signed in Cairo in May 1994 between Israel and the PLO, would lead to an independent Palestinian state; a similar proportion endorsed the agreement; and slightly less than one-fifth thought that the agreement would facilitate their return to pre-1948 Palestine. Half expressed the view that the agreement would not lead to an independent state, and about two-thirds said that they did not support the agreement and did not see it as implementing their right of return.

The highest level of support for the Israel-PLO accords came from older refugees (those above 50 years of age) and those in the highest income bracket. The younger age groups in Sha'ban's sample, particularly those between eighteen and thirty years of age, and those in the middle and low income brackets opposed the agreement in greater numbers and did not think it would give them the right of return or lead to an independent Palestinian state.

When asked to assess their relationship with the PLO before and after the signing of the Gaza-Jericho accord, three-quarters rated the relationship as "bad" in the wake of the agreement, compared to only 41 percent who thought the relationship was "bad" prior to the agreement. Among the poorest refugees, only 14 percent rated the relationship as "good" subsequent to the signing of the agreement. Although few suggested an alternative to the PLO as an organization to represent them, more than half of the sample felt that it was acting independently of the wishes of the Palestinian people. Nevertheless, more than half continued to consider the PLO as the sole representative of the Palestinian people. When asked to choose a leader for the PLO from a list of names, 37 percent did not choose anyone in particular, 22 percent of the sample chose Yasir Arafat, and the rest named other individuals.

Seventy percent of the refugees in Sha'ban's sample opposed resettlement in Lebanon, and 82 percent said that they would like to live in Palestine in the future. Only 8 percent chose Lebanon as their first choice of future residence. However, when asked to choose a country of residence in the event that they could not return to their original homes,

45 percent named Lebanon, 20 percent Europe, 6 percent the Americas, and 6 percent named other Arab countries. Fifteen percent did not choose any country. Around half of the well-to-do refugees and the older groups named Lebanon as their preferred country, if they were not allowed to return to Palestine. The majority of the young and educated rejected Lebanon as a place for permanent settlement.

In her survey of Palestinian refugee camps in 1991, Basma Kodmani-Darwish (1994) studied a total of 406 respondents: 150 from Jordan (Wihdat, Jabal el-Hussein, Jarash, Zarqa, Martyr, and Baqa'a camps, in addition to interviews with Palestinians from Amman, Wadi el-Sir, Zarka, Irbid, Soueileh, and Al-Aghwar) and 256 from Lebanon (100 respondents from the Beddawi and Nahr el-Bared camps in the north, 78 respondents from Ein el-Hilweh camp in the south, and a similar number from Bourj el-Barajneh camp in the center of the country). Kodmani-Darwish's main findings may be summarized as follows: (1) the Palestinians had undergone a process of "Lebanonization;" about 80 percent of them mentioned Lebanon as their birthplace. This is a population well into its third generation as refugees; (2) very few had family members living in the occupied territories, but between one-third and one-half said they had relatives in Israel. This reflects the fact that almost all of Lebanon's refugees came from the Galilee region of northern Palestine; (3) by an overwhelming majority, the Palestinians in Lebanon ranked the intifada as the most important Palestinian event in recent times, and between one-half and two-thirds preferred to see it continue as an armed struggle; and (4) despite their skepticism about the peace talks, they continued to regard the PLO as a salient and representative body, though respondents from the south endorsed the PLO with less enthusiasm than respondents from the other two regions in the survey. At the same time, the south, which is more exposed to Israeli attacks and factional conflicts, over-whelmingly approved the 1988 Palestine National Council declaration in essence calling for a two-state solution.

As for attitudes about the right of return, about 50 percent of Kodmani-Darwish's respondents said they would choose to live in the West Bank and Gaza. However, this was more a product of necessity than free choice, with around one-third attributing this choice to their possible expulsion from Lebanon. However, even for those who chose not to live in the new Palestinian entity, the majority would want to exercise their right to establish residency there, even on a temporary basis, and to obtain a Palestinian identity card. A clear consensus emerged with regard to the right of return, with more than 90 percent saying that exercise of their right of return was essential for settling the conflict, as a matter of principle and justice.

As already noted, the Palestinians in Jordan enjoy substantial rights by comparison with those in Lebanon. They have the right to work, to own property, and to obtain a passport, and the majority can partake in the country's political life. Still, there is tension between Jordanians and Palestinians, and the social distance separating Palestinians from Jordanians emerges clearly from Kodmani-Darwish's survey. Only 13 percent of the Palestinians she surveyed felt very close to Jordanians, compared to 50 percent who felt close to Palestinians in the occupied territories. One-third of the Palestinians questioned said they would remain in Jordan under any circumstances. Only 6 percent said that the situation in Jordan was unbearable enough to make them want to leave. Thirty-seven percent saw Jordan as a substitute state, whereas 49 percent rejected the proposition. However, 56 percent endorsed the idea of Palestinian-Jordanian confederation.

To the question "Must Israel be recognized?", 84 percent answered in the negative, and 64 percent said they could not see themselves living with the Israelis. Fifty-six percent approved of the PLO's political strategy of negotiating the future of the territories, yet fully three-quarters of the sample identified with the intifada. Forty-five percent of the sample saw the PLO's preoccupation with the future of the territories as being carried out at the expense of the refugee issue. This response was echoed in the finding that only 40 percent of the respondents thought that the establishment of a Palestinian state constituted a comprehensive solution to the Palestinian problem. However, should a Palestinian state come into being, 77 percent expressed their desire to live in it. This desire was guided mainly by moral considerations and "principle," and not by hostility toward Jordan or dissatisfaction with life there. Seventy percent saw free access to their homeland in Palestine as a necessity in any future agreement between the Palestinians and Israel.

Tension between Palestinians and Jordanians came to the surface again after Jordan concluded a peace treaty with Israel in September 1994. Opposition to the treaty was not, however, confined to Palestinians, but was also present among Jordanians (Brand 1995, 59). These findings are in contrast to a recent Jordanian survey that discovered that 95 percent of camp refugees believed that Jordanian-Palestinian relations were good, and a similar proportion endorsed closer relations between

Jordan and a future Palestinian state (Jaber 1996).

One of the very few systematic studies of refugee attitudes in the West Bank and Gaza was carried out in May 1995 by the Center for Palestine Research and Studies (CPRS) in Nablus. The survey asked a random sample of 1,271 respondents eighteen years of age and older from the West Bank (856) and Gaza (415) their views on the future of the camps. Forty-seven percent said that the camps should remain where they were but that living conditions should be improved. Close to 20 percent preferred to keep the camps as they were, and 25 percent suggested moving the camp residents to other localities. About 6 percent had no opinion on the subject. It is significant that almost 75 percent of the sample preferred to keep the camps where they were, with the majority calling for improvement in the physical conditions of the camps (CPRS 1995, 10).

In June 1995, the JMCC polled 1,397 Palestinians in the West Bank and Gaza on various issues pertaining to the performance of the PA. Included in the survey was the following question: "Do you agree [to] giving up the 1948 lands in return for a final solution stipulating a Palestinian state in the West Bank and Gaza Strip, with Jerusalem as its capital (the 1967 borders)?" Thirty one percent answered in the affirmative and 60 percent in the negative, with the remainder undecided. West Bank and Gaza respondents hardly differed on this score.

More significant were differences according to age and political affiliation. Forty-one percent of Fateh supporters approved of relinquishing claims to 1948 Palestine, whereas only 17 percent of Hamas supporters answered in the affirmative. When broken down by age, the younger generation reacted more negatively to the above question than the older one. Fully 66 percent of those who were born after 1967 opposed forfeiting the 1948 lands for an independent state with East Jerusalem as its capital, compared to 55 percent of those who were born before 1967. Further analysis of the data by the author revealed that the youngest cohort in the sample, those between fifteen and eighteen years of age, expressed the greatest opposition to relinquishing claims to the 1948 lands. Around 70 percent opposed the proposition, 26 percent approved it, and the remaining 4 percent had no opinion on the subject (JMCC 1995, Table 13).

3 | Israeli Approaches to Refugees

Having examined the status of Palestinian refugees in the Arab countries and the attitudes of the refugees themselves, we now consider Israeli, Palestinian, and other approaches to the refugee issue. Specifically, this discussion will focus on the right of return, modalities of refugee compensation, and various schemes of absorption and resettlement.

The Israeli position has remained more or less tied to its established position vis-à-vis the return of the 1948 refugees, with Labor showing only slightly more flexibility on the issue than Likud. This is in contrast with the Palestinian position on the 1948 refugees which, in actual if not in declaratory terms, has evolved substantially over the last two decades to reflect an overall change from long-standing rejection of the Jewish state and insistence on the literal interpretation of Resolution 194 to more flexible approaches based on mutual recognition.

As a prelude to summarizing Israeli approaches to the right of return, it is worthwhile to review the main ingredients of this position. Except for two limited offers in mid-1949 that came to nothing--one to take control of Gaza back from Egypt and settle the refugees already there and another to take back 100,000 of the refugees to be settled in places of Israel's choosing (Morris 1987, 266-85)--Israel has made no significant proposal to repatriate 1948 Palestinian refugees. For nearly fifty years, Israel has consistently refused to deal with the issue except in the context of an overall settlement of the Arab-Israeli conflict, which it knew full well was a nonstarter whenever it was raised.

Israel's agreement to pay compensation to the 1948 refugees has been conditional. For example, during 1949-1950. Israel claimed that the payment of compensation should be calculated not individually but on a global basis, with the payment of a lumpsum to resettle the refugees in the host countries to be raised internationally and administered by an international organization. This remains Israel's position to this day. Israel also insists that the loss and damage of property incurred by Jews during the 1948 war should enter into the calculations as well. By the mid-1950s, Israel linked compensation of Palestinian refugees to an end to the Arab boycott, the conclusion of comprehensive peace with the Arab governments, and compensation for Jews from Arab countries who settled in Israel. The acceptance of these demands was a remote possibility at the time they were made and was used by Israel as a pretext for creating facts on the ground in the interim period through confiscating Arab property, preventing the refugees' return, and bringing in new Jewish immigrants. This pattern has continued into the 1990s in the occupied territories, even though Israel has signed a peace agreement with the Palestinians and its relationship with many Arab countries is on the way to normalization.

Official Approaches

Commenting on the recent official Israeli position regarding the refugee issue, Shlomo Gazit (1994) noted that it was

> surprising to observe the almost utter indifference to the Palestinian refugee problem exhibited across nearly the entire spectrum of the Israeli political establishment. Instead of giving the issue a high priority at the multilateral talks, Israel has seemed unconcerned. Instead of being the interested party, urging pursuit of a solution, instead of raising it at the Oslo and Cairo negotiations, instead of forcing the Palestinians to adopt a realistic approach, Israel did its best to avoid discussion. (p. 12)

Although Gazit is correct insofar as Israel has consistently refused any discussion of its own responsibility with regard to the refugee problem, it has never been short on plans to resettle the refugees in neighboring countries. The fact that no such resettlement has taken place is due to several factors, including the refugees' determination to return to their homes, the unwillingness of the Arab governments to absorb them, and the emergence of the PLO as a national organization dedicated to regaining Palestinian rights.

On 5 June 1948, Joseph Weitz, director of the Jewish National Fund, met with David Ben-Gurion, Israel's first prime minister, and suggested a plan for preventing the return of the Palestinian refugees to their homes.

According to Abu Samra (1992), this plan consisted primarily of creating facts on the ground that would make the refugees' return impossible. The plan consisted of (1) destroying the largest possible number of Arab villages through military operations; (2) preventing the Arabs from ever working their deserted land, including sowing and harvesting the fields; (3) preventing the creation of a "vacuum" by settling Jews in a number of Arab towns and villages; (4) passing laws to prevent the return of the refugees; (5) mounting a campaign of propaganda to prevent the return of the refugees; and (6) helping the Arab countries absorb the refugees (see also Masalha 1992).

Ben-Gurion approved all the elements suggested except the last, which was not compatible with his priorities at the time. He addressed the issue in some detail at a meeting on 26 August 1948, stating that the Palestinian refugees should not be allowed to return because they would constitute a fifth column. The Arab countries should look after them. If Israel were pressured by the international community to return the refugees, it should resist this pressure. If forced, Israel would allow the return of a limited number of skilled urban dwellers, but it would not permit the return of any villagers (Abu Samra 1992).

A few weeks earlier, Moshe Shertok (later "Sharett"), Israel's first foreign minister, had rejected the recommendations for a refugee return made by Count Folke Bernadotte, the UN mediator sent to Palestine to "promote a peaceful adjustment of the future situation of Palestine" and to "ensure the safety and well-being of the population" (United Nations General Assembly Resolution 186 (S-2) of 14 May 1948). Israeli writer Shamay Cahana (1993) summarizes Sharett's rejections as follows:

Israel feels for the pain and suffering of the refugees. However, in spite of this and due to security considerations and concern "for the stability of future peace prospects," Israel cannot agree to their return. Any repatriation, which is made on a humanitarian basis but ignores military, political and economic considerations, will miss its objective and adds further difficulties. The return of thousands of uprooted Arabs, while the war is still raging, will bestow military advantage on the attacking states and will harm Israel. The cause of the refugee problem is the refusal of the Arab League to recognize Israel's right to exist. (p. 11)

A month later, in September 1948, Count Bernadotte was assassinated in Palestine by the dissident Stern group led by Yitzhak Shamir, who later became prime minister of Israel. Bernadotte's recommendations, which cost him his life, made their way into UN Resolution 194 (III) with some modifications. In his original report Bernadotte called on Israel to facilitate the return of the refugees "at the earliest possible date" (Peretz 1993, 70). In contrast, Resolution 194 (III) stated that the "refugees wishing to return to their homes and live at peace with their neighbors should be permitted to do so at the earliest practicable date." As is shown below, Israeli writers and their supporters have made much of this distinction between the words "possible" and "practicable" and have interpreted the final text of Resolution 194 (III) as nonbinding and nonspecific with regard to the right of return.

Al-Zaru (1991) showed that almost twenty official Israeli plans dealing with Palestinian refugees--first the 1948 refugees and later those of 1967--were submitted between 1948 and the late 1980s. Moshe Sharett's proposal, made in 1956 during a visit to the United States, expressed Israel's readiness to consider the principle of compensation on condition that the refugees be settled in the host countries. In 1965, Prime Minister Levi Eshkol presented a plan to the Knesset calling for diverting aid to countries in the region in order to settle the refugees in them.

Between 1967 and 1987, the start of the intifada, no less than a dozen proposals were put forward to deal with the refugees in the occupied territories and elsewhere. They included the following:

• Proposals submitted in 1967 by Raanan Weitz, director of absorption in the Jewish Agency from 1963 to 1984, called for uprooting some of the refugees in Gaza and the West Bank to new locations in the West Bank.

• Abba Eban's proposal of 1968, made during a speech delivered at the United Nations, called upon the governments of the region to implement a five-year plan whose purpose would be to establish peace and settle the refugees in the Arab countries.

• In 1971, Ariel Sharon, who was the military commander in charge of Gaza at the time, embarked on a program of moving more than 40,000 refugees in the Gaza Strip to new locations (see also Aner 1984).

• In 1973, Israel Galili, then a minister in the Labor government, put forward a plan that called for rehabilitating the refugees by providing them with houses adjacent to the camps and by converting the camps into towns or amalgamating them with neighboring municipalities.

• The election platform of the Likud in 1975 proposed settling the refugee problem on the basis of an "exchange" of people and property between Palestinian refugees and Jewish immigrants from Arab countries.

In 1982, the Begin government appointed a ministerial committee headed by Mordechai Ben-Porath, an Iraqi Jew who now heads the World Organization of Jews from Arab Countries (WOJAC), to look into refugee questions. It came up with the most detailed plan to integrate the refugees in the West Bank and Gaza in neighboring towns through the removal of twenty-eight camps and the uprooting of some 250,000 camp residents. Israel estimated the cost of the project at close to $2 billion, to be raised from the United States and the Europeans. This was by far the most ambitious plan, but nothing came of it because of Israel's protracted involvement in Lebanon and widespread opposition of the refugees, who learned of the plan from the Israeli press.

In addition to discussing the plans mentioned by Al-Zaru, Zvit Steinboim's *The Palestinian Refugees: Portrait and Possible Solutions* (1993) provided more details about Ben-Porath's "rehabilitation" project. Refugees living under Israeli control were to be assisted in building new houses located near their camps, with the assumption that those who built their own homes would not be tempted to join guerrilla activities. Ben-Porath's plan consisted of the following elements, to be carried out in phases over a five-year period:

• building new houses for camp residents in stages. Five percent of the population would be housed during the first year, 15 percent during the second year, 25 percent the third year, and 30 percent during each of the fourth and fifth years;

• giving an independent municipal status to the new housing settlement;

• giving land and aid under the motto "build your own home" in accordance with an overall plan;

• unifying health and social services in the West Bank and incorporating in stages UNRWA's educational services into existing governmental educational institutions; and

• ensuring the overall coordination of the project with UNRWA.

The intifada saw yet another series of proposals for dealing with the refugee issue. During a visit to the United States in 1989, Prime Minister Yitzhak Shamir called for the convening of an international conference to solve the refugee issue. Israel, he declared, would contribute expertise and ideas to the project, and the United States, the Arab countries, and the international community could fund it. Shamir's ideas were similar to those of Yitzhak Rabin, then minister of defense in the national unity government, who proposed removing camps that posed a security threat to Israel's control of the territories. Moshe Arens, who succeeded Rabin, also called on the United States to head a campaign to raise $2 billion in order to resettle the refugees.

With regard to the so-called Arab question, the Likud remained faithful to the historic stance of its precursor Herut, the revisionist right-wing party within the Zionist movement. On 31 October 1991, Shamir told delegates to the Madrid conference that the "Land of Israel is our true homeland" and that "any other country, no matter how hospitable, is still a Diaspora, a temporary place on the way home." Quoting from Mark Twain's travelogue while visiting the Middle East, he went on to dismiss other claims to Palestine. "To others," Shamir said, "it was not an attractive land; no one wanted it." In rejecting the legitimacy of Palestinian and refugee claims to Palestine, Shamir repeated the familiar official Israeli charge that the Palestinians were urged to leave by their leaders and that Arab governments were to blame for keeping the refugee issue alive by refusing to dismantle the camps and absorb their inhabitants (Shamir 1991). Not long after this speech, Shamir told *The Jerusalem Post* on 14 May 1992 that the "Palestinians' right of return will never happen" (cited in Takkenberg 1995, 2).

In October 1994, the Israeli government published a background paper on the refugee issue outlining well-known positions it had reiterated regularly since 1948:

• The 1948 refugee problem was the creation of neighboring Arab states.

• Close to 600,000 Jewish refugees had to flee Arab countries in the early 1950s and seek shelter in Israel.

• The number of displaced Palestinian refugees in the 1948 and 1967 wars was less than that claimed by the Arab side. According to Israeli figures, between 540,000 and 720,000 Palestinians were made refugees in 1948, and about 250,000 became refugees as a result of the 1967 war.

• The definition of refugee according to UN Resolution 194 (III) was imprecise and at variance with other international legal definitions of refugee status. For example, the 1948 International Declaration of Human Rights and the 1966 International Covenant on Civil and Political Rights related to individuals and not to a displaced collectivity of people (Government of Israel 1994).

The Israeli background paper emphasized a point to be discussed later, namely that

according to these same international documents, the right of return belongs to nationals, or at least permanent residents, of a state. The Palestinian refugees have never been nationals or permanent residents of Israel; they either fled before the establishment of the State in 1948, or before the areas where they lived came under Israeli control in 1948 or 1967. (Government of Israel 1994, 10)

The government paper also reproduced a statement made by David Ben-Gurion on 1 August 1948, in which he outlined Israel's enduring policies toward the refugees:

When the Arab states are ready to conclude a peace treaty with Israel, this question [of refugees] will come up for constructive solution as part of the general settlement, and with due regard to our counter-claims in respect of the destruction of Jewish life and property, the long-term interest of the Jewish and Arab populations, the stability of the State of Israel and the durability of the basis of peace between it and its neighbors, the actual position of the Jewish communities in the Arab countries, the responsibilities of the Arab governments for their war of aggression and their liability for reparations, will all be relevant to the question of whether, to what extent, and under what conditions the former Arab residents of the territory of Israel should be allowed to return. (Government of Israel 1994, 5)

Addressing the RWG for the first time in November 1992, the head of the Israeli delegation repeated the official position by calling a "travesty" the proposition that the "Palestinian refugee problem [was] the result of mass expulsion." However, he went on to say that "the Palestinian refugee problem was born as the land was bisected by the sword, not by design, Jewish and Arab. It was largely the inevitable by-product of Arab and Jewish fears, and the protracted bitter fighting" (Ben-Ami 1992, 3). This language, echoing Israeli historian Benny Morris's well-known formulation that the refugee problem was "born of war, not of design," represents an important departure in Israeli official thinking, even though it is overlaid with the symmetry of culpability and will likely not impress those who have languished for generations in camps, whether they were actually expelled from their homes or left for fear for their lives. Still, the statement does acknowledge some Israeli responsibility in what the head of the Israel delegation to the RWG called "the inherent immorality of the war" (Ben-Ami 1992, 5).

In an interview with the newspaper *Ha-Aretz* in July 1994, then Deputy Foreign Minister Yossi Beilin, generally known as a dove in Israeli Labor government circles, referred to Resolution 194 (III) as only "symbolically significant" for Israel and for the Arabs, including the Palestinians. Whereas Beilin's main concern was to dilute Resolution 194 (III), former Israeli prime minister Yitzhak Shamir was more direct in commenting on the Palestinian right of return. For Shamir,

[t]he term "right of return" is an empty phrase that is utterly meaning-less . . . . It will never happen, in any way, shape or form. There is only a Jewish "right of return" to the land of Israel. (cited in Takkenberg 1995, 2-3)

After the PLO and Israel signed the second agreement in Washington, DC, on 28 September 1995, Joel Singer, a legal advisor to the Israeli foreign ministry, published a detailed paper reflecting his "personal" views regarding the meaning of the agreement, in particular the limitations it placed on the Palestinian Council's jurisdiction. The paper made no mention of the refugees, other than to note that they would be dealt with in the final status talks (Singer 1995). However, when the final status talks did open in Taba, Egypt on 5 May 1996, the remarks by Uri Savir, the director general of the Israeli foreign ministry, omitted any reference to them (Savir 1996). Moreover, the press reported that the leading Palestinian representative at the meeting, Mahmud Abbas, refrained from mentioning the refugees in his speech, as requested by Israel (Al-Hasan 1996).

Semiofficial Approaches: Shlomo Gazit

Israeli writers whose research addressed the refugee issue have concluded, without exception, that the right of return mentioned in General Assembly Resolution 194 (III) is not sanctioned by international law, does not have the meaning and implication attributed to it by the Palestinians, and is impractical to implement and must be rejected because it means a fundamental transformation, if not the destruction, of Israel as a Jewish state.

Shlomo Gazit's report, *The Palestinian Refugee Problem* (published in 1994 by the Jaffee Center for Strategic Studies at Tel-Aviv University) drew the attention of commentators because its author is a retired army general with a military intelligence background and a close friend of the late prime minister Yitzhak Rabin. The report was given added weight when its author was appointed as an advisor to the Israeli multilateral teams, with special reference to refugee issues. Because of the importance of the report, it is discussed in some detail below.

When dealing with the right of return, Gazit made the point that except for the "brief episode in 1949, . . . [t]he political establishment is unanimous in denying the 'right' of return to Israel" (Gazit 1994b, 12) Moreover, he stated, "Israel's position is very clear: the option of 'return' should, under no circumstances, be provided to the Palestinians" (p. 13). Should Israel allow a small number of returnees back, the Palestinians must have no role to play in deciding their numbers or the modalities of return. The criteria of admission are basically humanitarian and are secondary to Israeli security claims and national interest. The return of Palestinian refugees in any significant number to Israel "will threaten the Jewish character of the state" (p. 14). In sum, "the return of the refugees would significantly worsen this delicate balance, increase the irredentist threat, and even endanger Israel's 1967 borders" (p. 14).

Gazit adopted UNRWA's definition of *Palestine refugees* but relied on Efrat's data to claim that UNRWA's figures should be reduced by 14 percent because of its originally inflated estimates. Gazit claimed that UNRWA's 1992 figure of 2.7 million registered refugees includes 800,000 Palestinians who are Jordanian citizens and should not be counted in the refugee global figure. He deducted them from the figure of 2.7 million and further reduced the balance of 1.9 million by 14 percent to come up with a final figure of 1.63 million refugees.

UNRWA has been criticized by the Israelis on many levels, with accusations ranging from its inaccurate counting and politicizing of Palestinian refugees to "institutionalizing" their status. Gazit claims that

> UNRWA institutionalized the refugees by using identification cards, establishing refugee camps with extra-territorial status separate from their local environment, and by regularly distributing food rations to all refugees. (Gazit 1994b, 4)

This theme, in which blame is put on UNRWA for keeping the refugee issue alive, forms part of the standard Israeli criticism of UNRWA (see Marx 1992).

Gazit singled out the Palestinians in Lebanon as being in need of assistance and viewed those in Jordan and Syria as being more or less integrated into their host societies. In his view, refugees in the West Bank and Gaza have been absorbed into the local economy, and once there is open passage between the two places, "the results of the free labor market will apply and help ameliorate the imbalance of the two areas" (p. 10). Once a Palestinian state is formed, Palestinians who might not want to return would also exercise their right to obtain a Palestinian passport.

Gazit (1994) argued that although the Palestinian leaders realize that it is unrealistic to exercise the right of return, this right should nevertheless be recognized in the abstract--thereby going beyond the official government stance. He was adamant, however, that

> [n]o doubt it would be dangerous for Israel to allow the refugees the freedom of choice between the realization of their "right" of return into Israel and their actual "return" to a future Palestinian state (with adequate compensation). (p. 11)

Successive Israeli governments since the 1950s have refused to pay compensation to the refugees, even though (according to Gazit) "Israel greatly benefitted from Arab property which came under its control, and which formed an important element in the infrastructure that enabled absorption of massive Jewish immigration after the 1948 War of Independence" (pp. 14-15). Gazit noted that Israel subsequently invoked its settling of Jewish refugees from Arab countries without asking for compensation from those countries. He believed that Israel was right to claim compensation for Jews from Arab countries while considering compensation to Palestinian refugees but did not believe that a successful settlement could be built on linking the two issues.

Gazit's views on the 1967 refugees were elaborated in a subsequent article published in the daily *Yediot Aharonot* (Gazit 1994a). He distinguished between the original inhabitants of the territories (i.e., the "permanent residents" of the West Bank and Gaza) who found themselves cut off from their homes as a result of the 1967 war, on the one hand, and the 1948 refugees who lived in the camps on the West Bank and Gaza and who became refugees for the second time because of the 1967 war, on the other. Gazit estimated that 280,000 people from the West Bank and Gaza became refugees, in addition to tens of thousands who had been outside the territories to study or work and were not allowed to return. Of the total number of displaced people, 70,000 were second-time refugees from 1948. Most of the rest had family members living in Jordan.

Taking into account natural increase, Gazit estimated the total number of 1967 displaced people and their descendants at between 500,000 and 600,000, after subtracting 88,000 who, he claimed, returned to the occupied territories between 1967 and June 1994. Gazit rejected the idea of allowing early return of second-time refugees, who will end up living in the West Bank and Gaza refugee camps for the third time. He argued that they must await the conclusion of the final status talks based on the Oslo Accord. He suggested that neither the Israeli government nor the Israeli public would object should the PA promise at a later stage to settle them in the former occupied territories over a five-year period.

With regard to the immediate return of the residents of the territories, he predicted opposition by Israeli groups, who would claim that the return of the 1967 refugees would lower the percentage of the settlers in the territories from 12-13 percent to 8-9 percent. As long as issues of final borders and the status of the refugees have not been settled, Gazit suggested that Israel should "reject any acts that might precipitate these discussions" about the refugees regaining their property, in case the property had been confiscated by the Israeli government for the sake of Jewish settlements. In any case, he maintained, the return of this group of 1967 refugees should not be an uncontrolled process; Israel should be assured that the local economy can integrate and absorb them.

Gazit summarized an assortment of American positions enunciated by unnamed senior U.S. officials. He stressed the close alliance and convergence between the positions of Israel and America, quoting especially President Nixon's commitment to Golda Meir in 1971 that the U.S. "will not pressure Israel to accept a solution that could undermine the Jewish character of the state and endanger its security" (p. 21). Gazit points out that the U.S., which had supported UN Resolution 194 (III) from the beginning, has recently "become more realistic" and has left the matter to be decided by the parties themselves.

After having concluded that the solution to the refugee problem does not depend on the right of return, Gazit argued that any solution would require the cooperation of the Arab host countries. The final status negotiations must include the refugee problem with all its ramifications. Gazit mentioned several demands that Israel ought to make of the Palestinians in this eventuality, namely that the Palestinians and the PA must (1) issue a "renunciation" of the right of return; (2) dismantle UNRWA in the Gaza Strip and West Bank; (3) abolish the special status of refugees; and (4) absorb and rehabilitate the refugees residing in the West Bank and Gaza. Moreover, it is expected that the PA will initiate a Palestinian law of return, which would entitle every Palestinian in the diaspora to return to the new Palestinian entity and obtain Palestinian citizenship. The Palestinians also must be willing to conclude a clear agreement with Israel on refugees once all other outstanding issues are resolved.

To placate the Palestinian refugees who will not be able to exercise their right of return to Israel proper, Gazit wanted Israel to issue a "moral-psychological acknowledgment" recognizing the suffering of the Palestinians in the last fifty years. Although Israel might not want to issue such a statement for fear of assuming culpability, Gazit believed it must do so. If Israel cannot bring itself to make an acknowledgement directly, he suggested that such a statement could come as part of an international resolution, like a new UN General Assembly Resolution which would be supported by Israel, and would welcome Palestinian-Israeli agreement on the refugee problem, recognize severe sufferings of the Palestinians, and commend their realism and readiness to enter into an intensive rehabilitation program for the refugees, while relinquishing their claim to "right of return" to Israel. Such a resolution would also replace article 11 of UN Resolution 194 (III), which presently serves as the basis for Palestinian political demands. (p. 30)

Gazit also called on Israel to assume its share of the financial burden of rehabilitating the Palestinians, the danger of culpability notwithstanding. He suggested that one source for the funds could come from Israel's $5-$10 billion claim against East Germany, now part of Germany. If Israel would agree to channel part of these reparations payments to rehabilitate the Palestinian refugees, Germany might be more eager to pay and thus be seen as contributing to a solution to the Middle East conflict. In addition to Israel's contribution, Gazit called on the rich Arab states and the industrialized countries to assume their share. Israel's involvement in this rehabilitation scheme would contribute toward a normalization of its relationship with the Palestinians; it would put its experience in refugee absorption into effect and would make sure that third parties made their contribution. If the Arabs reject such direct and open Israeli participation, then it could be part of an international rehabilitation effort.

Gazit argued that if the Palestinians remain unwilling to abandon their claims under UN Resolution 194 (III), despite Israel's issuing of a statement which carries moral-psychological significance, the PA should dismantle UNRWA, continue to provide help for the needy on an individual but not on a collective basis as has been the case with UNRWA, provide housing, and create employment opportunities. As part of its bilateral agreement with Arab countries (in particular with Jordan, Syria, and Lebanon), Israel would ask that the refugees be integrated in those countries. If some Palestinians were deported by the host countries in the past, they should be allowed to return to the West Bank.

The international rehabilitation effort would also undertake a census of Palestinian refugees. Refugee compensation would be directed toward the building of houses, vocational training, and labor-intensive economic enterprises. UNRWA would be dismantled in the host countries once this international authority for rehabilitation is put in place. Compensation should be given at a fixed price of approximately $10,000 to each family and would not be based on the true value of property left in 1948.

Gazit concluded his paper by outlining several scenarios. First, if both parties refuse to yield on their demands regarding the law of return, then either the talks would be suspended or the parties should move on to other subjects in the hope that their positions will be modified in the interim period. Second, a change in government in Israel from Labor to Likud could result in the actual rolling back of the agreement concluded so far. Third, a refusal by the host Arab countries to cooperate in rehabilitating the refugees could prevent the peace process from achieving its longer term goals, but would not prevent the Palestinians and Israelis from continuing their bilateral talks. Fourth, the eruption of violence along the Israeli-Lebanese border could put the whole peace process in jeopardy. Finally, the use of *quid quo pro* between Palestinian property and Jewish property in the Arab world, though "justified," would not contribute to overcoming the Palestinian-Israeli impasse.

Nonofficial Approaches: Other Writers

Legal and Economic Approaches

In the following discussion, we examine a number of Israeli writings that offer legal and economic analyses of the right of return and compensation for the refugees. These approaches are supplemented with an overview of anthropological-sociological studies of refugee camps carried out by Israeli social scientists. One of the earliest writers to deal with this issue was Ruth Lapidoth, a law professor at Hebrew University. She advanced the familiar Israeli interpretation (summarized at the beginning of this chapter) that rejects the applicability of Resolution 194 (III) on the grounds that "[t]he Palestinian Arab refugees have never been nationals or permanent residents of Israel: they either fled before the establishment of the state of Israel in 1948, or before the areas where they lived were occupied by Israel in 1948 or 1967" (Lapidoth 1986):

[T]he right of return is an individual right that does not apply to displaced masses of people. Last but not least, the general limitation of the clause of Article 29 of the [1948 Universal] Declaration [of Human Rights] permits the non-application of the right; the influx of more than one and a half million mostly hostile refugees would without doubt "violate the freedoms of others" in Israel, and it would damage "public order and the general welfare in a democratic society." (p. 114)

To those who would criticize Israel's 1950 Law of Return as being discriminatory against non-Jews, Lapidoth replied that the Law favors (Jewish) groups but excludes none. This does not, of course, address the question why this right should be given automatically to masses of people who were neither residents nor citizens of the country and simultaneously denied to the original inhabitants; the same reasoning that Lapidoth invoked to disqualify the legitimacy of the Palestinian right of return could also be used to disqualify the Jewish right to return to what became Israel, a country of which Jews were not previously citizens.

Lapidoth applied the same logic of nonreturn to the 1967 refugees. In her interpretation, UN Security Council Resolution 237 of 14 June 1967 (Tomeh 1975, 142) called on Israel "to facilitate the return" and not to grant the "right" of return to the refugees. After dispensing with the applicability of the Universal Declaration of Human Rights to the Palestinian case, she interpreted the 1966 International Covenant on Civil and Political Rights as also denying the Palestinian refugees the right of return on similar grounds. However, with respect to Israel's Law of Return, Lapidoth (predictably) found no inconsistency between it and any of the existing international instruments.

More recent legal assessments of the right of return and compensation are advanced by Benvenisti and Zamir (1995) and by Tadmor (1994), who followed in Lapidoth's footsteps. The former study distinguished between various legal categories of individuals and properties owned by both Arabs and Jews. Thus, on the Arab side, there are the 1948 refugees, the 1967 refugees, and the so-called "present absentees." The latter refer to a minority among the 1948 refugees who either were internally displaced during the 1948 war, or who were allowed to return to Israel under a family reunification program immediately following the end of hostilities but who remained classified as absent according to the 1950 Absentee Property Law. According to Benvenisti and Zamir (1995), the law defined as absentee

a person who, at any time after November 29, 1947, was a national or citizen of one of the Arab countries fighting against Israel, or was in one of those countries, or had left his or her ordinary place of

> residence in Eretz Yisrael (Palestine) for a place outside Eretz Yisrael or for a place in Eretz Yisrael held at the time by forces that were fighting against the State of Israel. (p. 300)

The annexation of East Jerusalem in 1967, deemed illegal under international law, highlighted a further contradiction in the 1950 Absentee Property Law. The unilateral annexation meant that, on the one hand, the residents of East Jerusalem were technically considered residents of Israel even though very few of them have applied for Israeli citizenship, but, on the other, they remained "absentees" according to the Absentee Property Law. The response to the anomaly created by the unilateral annexation was to enact the 1973 Absentee Property (Compensation) Law, which gave East Jerusalem residents and Palestinian "absentees" living in Israel proper the right to seek compensation. Very few Palestinians took advantage of the compensation offer, possibly because the offer was small and they did not wish to jeopardize their rights in any future settlement by bestowing legitimacy on Israeli actions.

An important reason for not returning abandoned property to its Arab owners, including property owned in West Jerusalem, is connected with the right of return. As Benvenisti and Zamir noted (1995):

> Unilateral recognition of the rights of these people to regain the property they had abandoned within Israel in 1948 might have constituted a precedent for recognizing a general Palestinian "right of return" (or at least a "right of repossession"), a very problematic issue. (p. 310)

On the Jewish side, nearly all of the private property owned by Jews was located in what became Israel, except for "thirty or forty square kilometers of land and several hundred buildings (mainly in the West Bank)" (p. 298). Jewish-owned property in the West Bank and East Jerusalem was not returned by Israel to its Jewish owners when the territory was seized, although compensation was paid, and the property was used for "public purposes" (i.e., to accommodate incoming Jewish immigrants).

Despite the insignificant size of Jewish property in the West Bank and Gaza and the vast tracts of Arab land in Israel proper (Jews owned only 7 percent of the land in Mandatory Palestine on the eve of the 1948 war), the authors saw a parallel situation between the state's refusal to return Jewish-owned land to its Jewish owners in the West Bank after 1967 and its similar treatment of Arab-owned land in Israel proper. The upshot of their analysis is that payment of compensation is preferable to exercising the right of repossession or return. This is born out by "history" as well as by past interpretations, such as Lapidoth's, and relevant international agreements, such as the Universal Declaration of Human Rights, the International Covenant on Civil and Political Rights, and even UN Resolution 194 (III). Repossession and right of return are more applicable to internally displaced refugees, the authors concluded. However, they did not address the predicament of the some 150,000 internally displaced Palestinian refugees within Israel.

The reference points for settling the entire Palestinian-Israeli dispute, according to Benvenisti and Zamir, are Resolutions 242 and 338, which, in the case of the former, referred to a "just settlement of the refugee problem" without mentioning the right of return. The authors saw a clear linkage between these resolutions and the 1993 Palestinian-Israeli agreement.

In accepting Security Council Resolutions 242 and 338 as the basis for a permanent settlement, the Israeli-Palestinian accords imply a territorial compromise in Palestine/Eretz Yisrael, and a rejection of a general right to return or repossess property in Israel. (p. 327)

After having dispensed with the right of return and property repossession, the authors concluded by describing modalities for compensation. First, they argued that compensation must be collective and not individual; it should have a global rather than a rights-based approach. Second, although it must rely on concrete proof of property ownership, the agreement should be based on lump sum payment. Third, payment should be equitable and dictated by present and future needs of the refugees; in other words, it should reflect the so-called "adequate compensation" and not the true value of property at the time of abandonment. Finally, the authors called for settling compensation claims by a mechanism that includes Arab governments, the PLO, Israel, and the international community.

Yoav Tadmor's (1994) legal approach to the issues of compensation and return was similar in essence to the Israeli approaches outlined so far. Repatriation of the 1948 refugees to Israel would not be allowed other than in "exceptional circumstances." For Tadmor, Resolution 194 (III) did not imply the right of return under international law, because it is informed by moral considerations and international customary law. As such, it is advisory in nature and not legally binding. "Principles of international law and equity," as they apply to Resolution 194 (III), relate to compensation and not repatriation. The Refugee Convention is of little help in furthering the Palestinian case because of UNRWA's sole jurisdiction over the refugees. In any case, the intentions of the Convention are not to facilitate repatriation but to provide protection from expulsion and to ensure that refugees are given treatment similar to that accorded to citizens of the host countries. The application of the Universal Declaration of Human Rights is rejected because it lacks legal force. Since the Declaration's application is contingent on safeguarding the integrity of the state, the return of masses of displaced Palestinian refugees to Israel will fundamentally change the character of the state and threaten public order.

How is it then, Tadmor asked, that Israel adheres to General Assembly Resolution 181 regarding the partition of Palestine which created the state of Israel, and General Assembly Resolution 173(III), which sanctioned Israel's admission to the United Nations with "unreserved" compliance with the UN Charter and its resolutions, yet it abstains from complying with General Assembly Resolution 194 (III)? After all, these are all nonbinding resolutions, according to Israeli interpretations. In other words, Israel selectively accepts some UN resolutions as binding and considers others to be nonbinding. The author did not give a satisfactory answer to this dilemma, other than to say that "Israel did not rely solely upon UN resolutions for its right to exist, and there are other factors which established that right" (p. 415).

Hebrew University economist Ruth Klinov (1995) focused mainly on compensation for Palestinian refugees. Three premises underlie her quantitative assessment: (1) although no ceiling is put on the number of refugees who are prepared to return to the West Bank and Gaza, many will choose to remain in their present locations; hence, the emphasis will be on rehabilitation; (2) Using the UNRWA data and the PLO's (1993) *Program for Development of the Palestinian National Economy for the Years 1994-2000*, she cited 500,000 as the number of expected returnees from the 1967 war between 1993 and 2000 and noted that more than 1,000,000 Palestinian refugees will continue to reside in Arab countries; and (3) the author assumed that the number of Palestinian refugees allowed to return to their homes in what is now Israel will be "negligible."

Klinov outlined four different approaches to calculating the amount of reparations and reached an overall sum that reflects a synthesis of three approaches. First, one can begin by identifying the donors and the extent and nature of the contributions that might be expected. Second, one can approach the amount of reparations in terms of the needs of the refugees as defined by UNRWA. A third approach would focus on regional investment and development, especially in four main sectors: housing, direct production, infrastructure, and human capital. The fourth approach would calculate the amount of reparations on the basis of the true value of Palestinian losses incurred as a result of the 1948 and 1967 wars. The last option was only mentioned briefly by the author and dismissed as unrealistic because "by all accounts the amount of past losses exceeds available resources by so much," and "in the majority of cases the difficulties in establishing title to lost property, and in assessing its worth, are insurmountable" (p. 4).

By beginning with an estimate of the amount needed to meet the housing requirements of the refugees (she adopted a figure of $20,000 per household), Klinov arrived at a total requirement of $2.56 billion to cover Palestinian refugees in Jordan, Lebanon, Syria, Gaza, and the West Bank. Although this investment will create employment in the process of building houses, it will leave very little money to be spent in other job-creating fields. Because her interest is in a "regional" settlement of the refugee issue, she warned against "squandering" a large chunk of refugee reparations in a short period or on immediate consumption. Instead, she argued that building houses in Gaza and the West Bank should be spread over 10-20 years. She was not averse to the return of 1948 refugees to the West Bank and Gaza and pointed out that those returning will bring their compensations with them. This may have a positive effect on the receiving regions but a negative impact on the sending ones.

Toward the end of her paper, Klinov cited three figures relating to the value of abandoned Arab property: (1) the Conciliation Committee for Palestine's (CCP) estimate of the value of agricultural plus nonagricultural property at about $1.85 billion in 1990 prices; (2) a figure in a recent study estimating the value of agricultural property in 1993 prices at between $2.3 and $2.8 billion; and (3) the amount in Hadawi's study, which estimated the value of agricultural, nonagricultural, and public property, including the projected increase in the value of property after 1948, at $11.5 billion at 1990 prices. Klinov favored two figures for reparations: a lower figure of $2 billion and an upper one of $4 billion. The lower figure is based on the amount of $2.6 billion pledged by the World Bank and mentioned by the RWG; the higher figure assumes further contributions from the international community. In addition to the two sets of figures, she took into account the need for the "rechanneling of UNRWA investment in education, vocational training, health, and social assistance, amounting to $250 million annually," which over ten years will bring in another $2 billion (p. 4).

By calculating the annual growth of investment in each of the regions under two scenarios (5 percent and 10 percent annual growth) over a decade (1995-2005), Klinov reached the conclusions that reparations will constitute (depending on whether the available sums of money for reparation are $2 or $4 billion) around 10.4 percent (lower figure) to 45 percent (upper figure) of investment in Jordan, a corresponding 15.2 percent to 70.6 percent of investment in the West Bank, 44.8 percent to 208 percent of investment in Gaza, and 7.3 percent to 57.6 percent for Lebanon. (Syria is excluded from the analysis due to lack of data on public and private investment.) In distributing the reparations, she recommended that between $3,700 and $7,000 be given to individual households and that the rest be administered by the authorities in question.

This survey of nonofficial Israeli approaches to the refugee question was concluded with a brief mention of historian Ronald Zweig's references (1993) to Israel's experience with German reparations payments as a possible model around which to fashion Palestinian refugee compensation. Zweig distinguished between restitution, reparation, and indemnification, defining *reparation* as "payments between states, usually as compensation for damage caused in war," *indemnification* as "payment to individuals as compensation for suffering and non-material losses (loss of education, health, etc)," and *restitution* as "the return of material assets to their rightful owners or heirs" (p. 57). Although German reparations for Nazi victims encompassed all three types of compensation, Zweig would consider compensating Palestinian refugees only in terms of collective restitution, that is, compensation for material losses.

Anthropological-Sociological Approaches

Israeli approaches to the Palestinian refugees are primarily concerned with resettling the refugee population either through dismantling the camps or amalgamating them with their surroundings. This is true for the camps in the West Bank and Gaza as well as the surrounding Arab countries. Any right of return is dismissed out of hand. After the 1967 war, one of the early projects on the refugee camps was sponsored by the Rand Corporation and carried out by anthropologist Emanuel Marx and economist Yoram Ben-Porath. The results were reported in *Some Sociological and Economical Aspects of Refugee Camps on the West Bank* (1971). With historian Shimon Shamir, the above authors published (in Hebrew) *A Refugee Camp on the Mountain Ridge* (1974), a study of the Jalazoun camp on the West Bank. Amnon Cartin, a geographer, published a study of refugee resettlement in the Eastern Ghor in Jordan (1992). Among these authors, Marx was the most persistent in pursuing work on Palestinians refugees, and his work influenced subsequent Israeli academic research on the subject. In the early 1990s, he published two articles, one in Hebrew that focused on the Gaza Strip (1991), and the other a review article that summarized previous work and reiterated his views on the subject (1992). More recently, anthropologist Joseph Ginat (1994) from Haifa University discussed various Israeli and non-Israeli studies on Palestinian refugees with a similar purpose in mind--to solve the refugee problem through resettlement.

Marx's work was straightforward. He asserted that the distinction between camps and noncamps has disappeared. "One of our major findings," he wrote, "was that the refugees had been integrated in the economy and that the camps were becoming urban working class neighborhoods" (1992, 282). Moreover, UNRWA must bear responsibility for the fact that the refugee numbers have "grown over the years and why so many people still live in 'refugee camps'" (p. 281). A third theme was the interplay between Palestinian identity, ethnicity, and refugeehood. In the 1970s, when UNRWA's services declined, Palestinian identity reasserted itself and the refugees were willing to substitute houses provided by the Israeli occupation forces for their refugee dwellings. However, in the long run "UNRWA and certain Arab states intentionally, and Israel unintentionally, provided numerous situations which brought to the fore certain elements in the refugee ethnic identity" (p. 293). This contributed to the fusion between refugee identity and Palestinian nationalism. Thus, in Marx's words, "to be [a] refugee now meant to be in the forefront of the Palestinian struggle for national independence. The refugee identity had merged, for the moment, with the Palestinian one" (p. 292). Finally, as part of his argument for resettling refugees in neighboring countries, Marx made the extraordinary statement that "the refugee freedom of movement and employment was never restricted in other Arab countries" (p. 284).

Marx's work on Gaza (1991) was similar in its thrust. He argued that (1) the camps must be considered part of the cities, and camp houses should not be destroyed but improved with a view to granting them municipal status; (2) Israel should not construct exclusive refugee communities to replace the camps, because this would contribute to maintaining the distinction between refugees and nonrefugees; (3) illegal buildings in the camps should be licensed and proper urban planning undertaken through standardization of infrastructure services inside and outside the camps; (4) compensation should be paid to those who lost their dwellings and property in the 1948 war; and (5) there is no room left for additional Jewish settlements in the Gaza Strip.

There are several problems with Marx's framework. One can hardly describe the disorganized, seasonal, and marginal labor force in the camps, either under Israeli control or in other locations such as Lebanon, as "working class." To do so would be to rob the concept of its sociological significance. It is more appropriate to label them "underclass." Not surprisingly, Marx leveled the standard Israeli criticism of UNRWA, accusing it of perpetuating the refugee problem. By contrast, Schiff's (1995) somber analysis of the agency produced a drastically different picture. Israeli social science writings on the Palestinians generally tend to subject them to identity deconstruction. For example, the tendency has been to engage in hair splitting as to whether the identity of Palestinians in Israel is Palestinian, Arab, Moslem, Israeli, or any combinations thereof. The same hair-splitting exercise is performed on Palestinian refugees, with the Israeli preference that the "Palestinian" identity would win over the "refugee" identity, as if the two were contradictory or mutually exclusive. Finally, Marx's comment about freedom of movement and work in the Arab countries must come as a surprise to many refugees, particularly those who live in Lebanon, Egypt, and those in the Gulf (see chapter 2), not to mention the West Bank and Gaza where closures, curfews, and other restrictions imposed by Israel have become the norm rather than the exception.

Ginat (1994), who is concerned with reaching a "constructive" solution to the 1948 refugee problem, shared Marx's views and extended them to the Palestinian refugees in Lebanon, whom he visited under the auspices of the 1982 Israeli invasion of Lebanon. He quoted from press reports that show the deep frustration felt by the refugees in Lebanon over the Oslo agreement. He argued that the exclusion of refugees from Lebanon among Palestinian negotiators was a mistake committed both by

Israel and the Palestinian leadership. It is this exclusion, he claimed, which contributes to their current bitterness and opposition to the peace process. The truth is quite different on this score. The Palestinian leadership was willing and tried to add Palestinians from the camps in Lebanon to its delegations, but the opposition came from Israel and the refugees themselves. Ginat claimed that the right of return is adhered to more by the older than the younger generations of refugees and that the latter "understand that reality is different" (p. 7), a finding that flies in the face of evidence produced in chapter 2. The camps are no longer perceived as temporary places of residence but as normal urban centers, which include nonrefugees as well, Ginat argued; thus, "[t]he refugee camps should be systematically and methodically turned into permanent settlements. The camps adjacent or close to towns should be annexed to the local municipalities. The camps away from towns should be turned into permanent settlements and given an independent municipal status" (p. 9). Finally, when citizenship rights are granted to the Palestinian refugees in Arab countries, they will develop a sense of permanence and stability. Here again Ginat seemed oblivious to the tremendous problems encountered in granting citizenship rights in Arab countries to nonnationals. Even in those instances where the refugees are entitled to apply for citizenship such as Jordan, Cartin (1992) demonstrated that resettlement of the refugees was carried out without jeopardizing refugee rights and registration with UNRWA. In spite of all this, the results of the Ghor experiment in resettling refugees were mixed. What is peculiar about this cluster of proposed solutions is that the refugees themselves nowhere are offered a choice of compensation or return or a discussion of these and other modalities. Like their government, Israeli social scientists seem to know what is best and "realistic" for the refugees and are not concerned with giving them a choice.

4 | Palestinian Approaches to Refugees

Official and nonofficial Palestinian approaches to the refugee issue in general and the right of return in particular have evolved from a rejection of anything short of full implementation of Resolution 194 to an adoption of an accommodating stance toward Israel. The crucial turning point in Palestinian thinking on this matter came in 1988 during the nineteenth session of the Palestine National Council in Algiers, which served as the culmination of events initiated by the PLO as early as the mid-1970s. Needless to say, this accommodating stance remains unacceptable to a segment of the Palestinian constituency and (as stated in chapter 2) is far from being shared by the refugees themselves. Thus, the Palestinians entered the multilateral discussions on refugees without any clear notion of how to reconcile their political objectives with the mandate of the RWG and the Madrid formula. Moreover, refugee compensation, modalities of return, and resettlement were left unarticulated at the official level. Several scenarios were advanced unofficially to deal with the right of return and its various corollaries.

From the outset, Arab governments held Israel responsible for creating the refugee problem and demanded that the refugees be repatriated to their homes. In their view, any compensation that is considered and accepted by the refugees must be calculated on an individual basis and reflect the true value of the loss incurred; these, according to Arab estimates, amounted to 2 billion Palestinian pounds. The Arab states also considered that the United Nations bore responsibility for the creation of Israel through the November 1947 Partition resolution, and consequently should share in the payment of compensation. The refugees, they argued, had to be represented in any negotiations concerning compensation. Finally, those who were not repatriated had to receive their share of the value of public property left behind (Cattan 1969, 73-88; Peretz 1995, 73-88).

The issue of Palestinian refugees figured prominently in the evolution of the political claims of pan-Arabism as a state ideology. Its foremost champions were Egypt's Gamal Abd al-Nasser and the Ba'thists in Syria and Iraq (each with its own brand of Ba'thism). The massive defeat in the June 1967 war, which signaled the demise of pan-Arabism, was the final proof of the failure of the Arab states to redress Palestinian grievances, regain the lost homeland, and implement the refugees' right of return.

Official Approaches

The evolution of Palestinian political goals, which began in the middle of the 1970s and culminated in the declaration of independence in Algiers in November 1988 and the mutual recognition of Israel in 1993, has been documented (e.g., R. Khalidi 1989). Suffice it to note that during the 1980s, Palestinian academics and political activists from inside and outside the territories began holding seminars and group encounters in Europe and North America with their Israeli counterparts from the peace camp. Although these meetings were labeled unofficial, they were sanctioned, if not encouraged, by the PLO, and they undoubtedly played a significant role in pushing the Palestinian position further along the road of concessions and mutual recognition. These meetings, dubbed as "confidence building" measures, became a kind of training ground for future participation by some of these same actors in real negotiations with Israel (see Said 1996, 32-91). The tangible results of such encounters were the clandestine meetings of the early 1990s between Israelis and Palestinians, including academics on both sides, as a prelude to the Oslo I agreement. A similar pattern appeared to be repeating itself with regard to the final status talks. Ze'ev Schiff, a correspondent of the Israeli daily *Ha-Aretz*, reported on 22 February 1990 that twenty such meetings were held during the last month of the Labor government to discuss issues such as Jerusalem, refugees, settlements, borders, and withdrawal of Israeli forces, and certain members of the earlier teams participated in them.

This evolution in Palestinian thinking led to acceptance of Security Council Resolutions 242 and 338 as the bases for future negotiations with Israel. Both of these resolutions intended to address the aftermath of the 1967 and 1973 wars, although Resolution 242 called for "achieving a just settlement of the refugee problem." The resolution left the definition of *refugee* intentionally vague. It could mean the 1967 refugees only, or it could encompass the 1948 and 1967 refugees. Israel clearly preferred the former interpretation, and the word *displaced* crept into the diplomatic jargon and is now used strictly to refer to the 1967 refugees. As far as the Palestinians were concerned, *refugees* meant all those affected by the wars with Israel, whether in 1948 or 1967; those who were prevented from returning to their homes after those wars; and those who were expelled from their homeland after Israel occupied the territories.

The Palestinian interpretation was made clear at the opening of the Madrid conference in November 1991. In the eloquent words of Haider Abdul Shafi (1991), the Palestinian delegation to the Madrid conference came to Madrid "to narrate our story." This story had the theme of dispersal and refugeehood woven into it. "As we speak," he said, "the eyes of thousands of Palestinian refugees, deportees, and displaced persons since 1967 are haunting us, for exile is a cruel fate: bring them home. They have the right to return" (p. 3).

Very little was accomplished during the first few months of negotiations that began at Madrid and then moved to other venues, primarily Washington, DC. Prime Minister Yitzhak Shamir later revealed that his tactic at Madrid had been to delay and keep the negotiations in a holding pattern so as to allow Jewish settlements to keep expanding. The 1992 elections in Israel, which brought Yitzhak Rabin into office, changed the course of negotiations and saw the agreements between the PLO and Israel concluded. The election of Benjamin Netanyahu and the statements made by him so far suggest that the Israeli government will revert to the Likud negotiating tactic adopted by Shamir.

The Madrid conference was followed up with a steering committee meeting in Moscow, which established several technical committees at the multilateral level, one of which was dedicated to the refugees. This in itself promised at least to place the refugee item, with all the vagueness surrounding it, on the agenda for discussion. Indeed, the Palestinian delegation used this forum to reiterate General Assembly Resolution 194 at each of the eight meetings that followed. Although very little was accomplished as a result of this reiteration (partly because of the structure of the RWG and its basis in consensus), the Oslo I agreement between the PLO and Israel in September 1993 distinguished between the 1948 refugees and those displaced in 1967. The latter would be dealt with in the Quadripartite Committee, which included Egypt and Jordan, and the former bilaterally between the PLO and Israel as part of final status talks.

Several observations can be made about the official Palestinian position on the refugees. It was based on the right of return, as explained by Abdul Shafi and in a paper published by the Palestinian Information Ministry (1995). The paper argued that the Arab countries are economically incapable of absorbing the refugees and that the majority of the refugees, including those in the occupied territories, would prefer to go back to their original homes in Israel. The paper raised an important point, based on several studies, which runs contrary to the accepted wisdom in the debate over refugees. The paper showed that a majority of the refugees surveyed saw no contradiction between wanting to see their living conditions improved in the camps and wanting to return to their homes. Furthermore, not enough thought was given to clarifying how adherence to Resolution 194 fit with the Madrid formula. The result of the insistence on a reference to Resolution 194 was the gradual dilution of the force of the Resolution, and mentioning it eventually became a sort of ritual. To avoid rancor and abide by the consensus rule, Palestinian reference to Resolution 194 in final RWG statements was routinely accompanied, at the insistence of Israel and the United States, with qualifications that some members agreed to and others did not. Finally, because the RWG was meant to address nonpolitical (i.e., humanitarian and technical) aspects of the refugee question (with the possible exception of the family reunification theme), the meetings of the group gradually devolved into a recitation of the various studies carried out by the shepherd members of the RWG, which included databases, public health, vocational training, child welfare, and family reunification. Even so, in this ostensibly nonpolitical context, disagreements surfaced on several fronts. The Palestinians saw in the RWG a forum to deal with concrete issues; though humanitarian in their essence, the issues nevertheless had a political dimension to them, such as family reunification. Also, and equally important, the Palestinians were unwilling to divorce improvements in the living conditions, such as building new homes for the refugees, from their political implications.

After meeting for three years (1992-1995), the Canadian government, which chaired the meetings of the RWG under its gavelholder Marc Perron, issued a "vision paper" in March 1995 in order to give the stalled meetings a new and fresh impetus. The paper presented a vision of the nature of the problems facing the RWG in its deliberations and possible means of addressing them. A better Middle East, Perron argued in his paper, would be one in which there are no refugees. How this was to be achieved was the problem confronting not only Perron but the international community as a whole. For a start, the paper advanced the notion that the "taboo" should be lifted and questions of refugee return and resettlement addressed. From the Palestinian vantage point, merely raising the problems in this forum represented an advance, although doubt was expressed that the RWG could address these volatile issues. Perron's paper called for additional studies to assess absorption (without specifying where) of the refugees (housing, employment, etc.). The Israelis, through their Foreign Ministry, let it be known that the paper transgressed the mandate of the RWG and that these issues would be addressed in bilateral and quadripartite fora at the proper time. The paper was shelved, and Marc Perron was appointed Canada's ambassador to Mexico and replaced by Andrew Robinson, who until recently had been Canada's ambassador to Jordan.

Robinson tried to resuscitate one central idea of the vision paper. Instead of talking about the so-called "taboo" subjects of resettlement (which is unacceptable to the Palestinians) or absorption (which is unacceptable to the Israelis, unless of course it is confined to the Arab countries), he seized the notion of "adaptation." If Perron's vision paper caused consternation among the Israelis, Robinson's adaptation notion triggered suspicion among Palestinians.

The Palestinian position with regard to adaptation was twofold: first, that adaptation be confined to the West Bank and Gaza and should be aimed primarily at the returnees, first from the 1967 war and later from the 1948 war; and second, that adaptation must not mean altering the legal status of the refugees. During the eighth RWG meeting in Geneva in December 1995, the first meeting attended by Robinson as gavelholder, the topic of adaptation was initially introduced without considering its impact on the status of the refugees. The Palestinian delegation raised the issue and insured that, in keeping with its statement during the plenary session at the opening day of the conference in Geneva, any projects aimed at adaptation must ensure that the legitimate rights of the refugees are protected. A statement to this effect was introduced in the final communique of the conference. Two months later, Robinson floated a paper on adaptation written by Jill Tansley (1996), a researcher at the International Development Research Center in Ottawa, an arm of the Canadian government. Tansley's paper responded to Palestinian concerns by stating that adaptation will focus on the West Bank and Gaza and that "any initiative undertaken as an adaptation strategy must be entirely without prejudice to the rights and future status of the Palestinian refugees" (p. 1). It remains to be seen if and how the rhetoric of adaptation is translated into concrete policies without violating the historic rights of Palestinian refugees.

Overall, the official Palestinian position appears reactive: It responds to crises and initiatives from the outside, but it lacks an articulated agenda and a clear position on the refugee issue. In all likelihood, unofficial approaches may assume greater importance in further developing the official Palestinian position on the refugee issue, if and when final status talks resume.

Opposition to Oslo

The Palestinians entered the Madrid, Washington, and Oslo negotiations with a series of concessions behind them. Reference to the 1948 refugees' right of return was ritually made by Palestinian spokespersons in all international fora, but this right had no concrete expression in any of the agreements signed between the Palestinians and Israel.

Opposition to Oslo I and the secrecy in which it was negotiated emanated from various quarters within the Palestinian movement, not to mention the Arab world. Key figures within the PLO voiced public criticism of Arafat's leadership style. The "rejectionists" included George Habash's Popular Front for the Liberation of Palestine (PFLP), Nayif Hawatmeh's wing within the Democratic Front for the Liberation of Palestine (DFLP), and the Islamists; furthermore, mainstream elements within the PLO, including Faruq al-Qaddumi, who headed the PLO's Foreign Relations Department in Tunis, refused to join Arafat and his associates upon returning to Gaza in the wake of Oslo I.

Further criticism was levelled against the PLO under Arafat's leadership from Palestinian intellectuals and activists in the West and in the Middle East. Criticisms in the Middle East came from refugee communities, primarily in Lebanon, the Islamists, and left-wing radicals who saw in the Oslo agreement total capitulation to Israeli dictates. In the West, Palestinian intellectuals who had been active in furthering the Palestinian cause, such as Edward Said of Columbia University, mounted a campaign of criticism against Arafat's authoritarian leadership in handling the negotiations. In a book that appeared in Arabic in 1994 and in English in 1996, Said directed his scathing attacks of Arafat to a wider Arab audience. In his attack on the current PLO leadership, he was careful to state that he did not oppose peace with Israel, as long as the process was premised on democratic principles and recognition of

Palestinian historic rights. A recent seminar organized by Palestinian intellectuals in Damascus, Syria offered similar criticism of the Oslo agreement, in particular its treatment of the refugee issue (Kayali 1996).

In addition to this split within the ranks of the PLO and its supporters, the "inside-outside" dichotomy within the Palestinian movement once again came into play. Critics on the "outside" were particularly disappointed that the Oslo Accord was vague on statehood, the fate of the 1948 refugees, Jerusalem, and the future of settlements. Belatedly, they adopted the strategy of adding their appointees to Palestinian delegations to the peace talks, as happened during the last two meetings of the RWG. In December 1994, Tunis sent Zuhdi Tarazi, at one time the PLO's representative in the UN, to attend the meeting in Antalya, Turkey, and in December 1995, Tunis sent Zakaria Abdul-Rahim, director general of the Repatriates' Affairs, to attend the multilateral meeting which was held in Geneva, Switzerland.

It became obvious that the "outside" critics' message with regard to the refugees centered on the fate of those who left in 1948. Tunis felt these people were being neglected in the ongoing bilateral and multilateral talks. Tarazi came to Antalya armed with copics of relevant UN resolutions on the Palestine question, in particular the refugee issue, and Abdul-Rahim insisted on the right of return in a speech delivered to the Plenary meeting in Geneva. However, it appears that Tunis's approach is unlikely to alter the course of events. The PLO "inside" appears to welcome participation from its "outside" elements as long as it comes in small doses and the organization is able to absorb the criticism.

Nonofficial Approaches

In three recent articles, Rashid Khalidi (1990, 1994) and Ziad Abu Zayyad (1994) put forth approaches that may reflect the dominant Palestinian position. For Khalidi (1990), the issue was

> to determine whether a symbolic acceptance that an injustice has been done to the Palestinian people, via acceptance of the right of return in principle, combined with an attempt to right it, via implementation of this right in some specific and clearly defined fashion, will satisfy a sufficient number of Palestinians, while remaining acceptable to a sufficient number of Israelis, to constitute a viable solution to this question. (p. 5)

The crux of the matter is to interpret the right of return in Resolution 194 (III) so as not to remain bound to a notion of absolute justice.

Such a formula can be found, according to Khalidi, by recognizing the "limitations" of Resolution 194 (III). First, the resolution offered Palestinian refugees the choice "not to return" in favor of compensation. Second, those who are allowed to exercise their wish to return to what is now Israel should agree, according to Resolution 194 (III), "to live at peace with their neighbors," by accepting Israeli sovereignty over one part of Palestine. Third, the return need not be to the homes from which the Palestinians were originally driven out, but to a Palestinian state that would be established elsewhere in former Mandatory Palestine. The last point is not so much an interpretation of Resolution 194 (III), which does call for the refugees' "return to their homes," as much as it is an interpretation by Khalidi of statements made by PLO officials.

Khalidi proceeded to outline the modalities for the application of the law of return. For the Palestinians in Jordan, whose number exceeds 1 million, their problem can be resolved by means of an arrangement whereby "the Palestinian state and Jordan are voluntarily linked in a confederation which includes open borders, an agreement on nationality and jurisdiction, and a form of economic union" (1990, 11). This will meet Palestinians' national aspirations by providing them with Palestinian nationality, while at the same time securing for them economic compensation. Other problematic groups are the Palestinians in Lebanon and those who were expelled from Kuwait. Khalidi suggested a combination of return of some Palestinians in Lebanon to the new state, a very limited number to Israel proper, and others to a Jordanian-Palestinian confederation.

In a subsequent article on the subject, Khalidi (1994) warned against a "cavalier treatment of history," which buries the refugee question, and with it the right of return, in obfuscated historical debate surrounding the conditions under which the refugees left their homeland. To say, as Israeli officials do, that the Israeli government is not responsible for the refugee question is to overlook recent Israeli revisionist history, not to mention overwhelming Palestinian research on the subject. Khalidi outlined five components of a solution of the problem:

(1) There must be "symbolic" rectification to the problem, and this could be accomplished by having Israel acknowledge throughout its institutions

(e.g., in the educational system and the military establishment) the injustice done to the Palestinians.

(2) The Israelis must acknowledge in principle that the Palestinians have the right of return, even though it is difficult to implement in practice. In line with this principle, Israel should allow the return to their homes of a "few thousand or tens of thousands" on a regulated basis. This controlled entry will target the 1948 Palestinian refugees who have relatives in Israel or whose land and homes are still available. Khalidi revived the 1949 figure of 100,000 and suggested that "there is no earthly reason why today an Israel at peace with its neighbors and bestriding the region like an economic colossus cannot make such a simple gesture" (1994, 24).

(3) Compensation should be paid to all Palestinians not wishing or unable to return to their homes. He cited several figures, ranging from $92 billion to $147 billion [as calculated by Hadawi and Kubursi (1988), whose work is summarized below], to his own suggestion of $40 billion on the basis of a payment of $20,000 to each refugee, encompassing "an arbitrary figure" of 2 million refugees.

(4) The new state of Palestine will be the state of all Palestinians irrespective of where they live; for the refugees (and others) this means granting citizenship rights in principle to all Palestinians to live in this state and hold its passport.

(5) The citizenship status of the Palestinians in Jordan must be regularized by granting them full citizenship rights as Jordanians or, in the case of a confederal arrangement, granting them Palestinian citizenship as citizens of the new Palestinian state. With regard to those in Lebanon (and Syria), a few would be allowed to return to their homes in Israel proper, others should be given Palestinian passports to enable them to travel abroad in search of work, but the majority would have to stay in Lebanon as holders of Palestinian nationality. This would lead to concrete improvements in their civil rights as residents of Lebanon.

Ziad Abu Zayyad (1994), a current member of the Palestinian Council, covered familiar terrain and advanced more or less the same arguments outlined above, although in less detail. He too distinguished between the principle and its implementation, as far as the right of return in UN Resolution 194 is concerned. In his view, Palestinians could enjoy the principle of the right of return to "Palestine as a national homeland" without literally returning to their actual homes, villages, and towns of pre-1948 Palestine.

> The circumstances under which the Palestinian refugees have lived since 1948, and the suffering which they have endured and are still enduring, have forced many of them to view their return as the acquisition of national independence and dignity, and not necessarily as a literal return. (p. 77)

Zayyad suggested that the Palestinian return would be facilitated by the enactment of "a Palestinian Law of Return" to attract immigrants to the newly created state, with few returning to Israel itself. He emphasized that this formula is applicable to the 1948 refugees only, whereas the 1967 refugees should all be permitted to return to their homes in line with Security Council Resolutions 237, 242, and 338.

Khalid Muhammad Al-Az'ar (1995) presented a wide-ranging analysis of the refugee situation in the context of the Middle East peace process and the refugees' conditions in the Arab countries. He viewed the U.S. abstention in December 1993 from supporting Resolution 194 (III) and the lack of direct reference to crucial UN resolutions regarding the 1948 refugees as the result of the unfortunate absence of formal participation by the United Nations in the current peace process. Al-Az'ar noted that after UNRWA's recent decision to transfer its operations to the PA, confusion reigned among Palestinian refugees regarding their future status in the Arab countries. The consequences of this decision were felt in Syria, where the authorities clamped down on the refugees' freedom of movement; Libya, which witnessed a worsening in the treatment of its Palestinian community; Jordan, which suspended the new electoral law until the refugee issue is finally resolved; and Lebanon, whose government refused to approve the repair of shelters for refugees in the camps for fear that this would lead to their permanent resettlement in the country.

Al-Az'ar advanced various scenarios bearing on the future of the refugees. The first scenario posited the return on an individual basis of a limited number of 1948 refugees. He dismissed this scenario because it deprives the refugees of real equality. By accepting this solution, he maintained, the "refugees exchange unequal status as refugees to unequal status as citizens in a state [Israel] which is not theirs" (p. 30). He also noted the refugees' opposition to this option; Israel emphatically rejects it as well.

Al-Az'ar's second scenario allowed for the return of Palestinian refugees either in limited or expansive manner to the new Palestinian entity. The advantages include a solution to the refugees' immediate basic problems such as shelter, food, and employment, as well as the problem of infringements of human rights by the host societies. Many of the displaced and refugees would approve of this plan in exchange for their present conditions. The disadvantage of this scenario is that it compromises the refugees' historic right of return. The author noted that this "will not solve the deep-rooted problem as understood by generations of refugees themselves, that is the return to their birthplace" (p. 31), although he claimed that the return to the Palestinian entity could be construed as one step in the direction of reviving the original idea of return.

The third scenario involved an "open return" to a Palestinian-Jordanian federation or confederation, as the case may be. This is premised on the notion that because Israel objects to the total return of the refugees in the "direction of historical Palestine," such an arrangement would make possible the absorption of 4 million refugees in a larger, combined territory. "It is not far fetched," he wrote,

> that the foreign and international community as well as Israel will accede to this scenario and express readiness to offer material and technical aid to resolve the problem. However, in the final analysis this scenario does not correspond to the real promise of return, neither does it address the historical rights as understood by the refugees, even though it does provide for a wider base from which to pursue [their] rights which the current situation is unlikely to deliver. (p. 32)

Al-Az'ar's fourth scenario consisted of an "open return" to a Palestinian-Israeli confederation, in which the historical rights of the Palestinians are addressed by means of a Palestinian-Israeli democratic entity. This scenario is very similar to what the Palestinians advanced in the early 1970s regarding the establishment of a unitary, secular, and democratic binational state for Arabs and Jews inside the territory of former Mandatory Palestine. This scenario, which permits the Palestinians to return, even if not to their original homes, makes possible the purchase of land in Palestine by those who do not wish to return and meets a great deal of Palestinian national aspirations. Needless to say, this last scenario has no chance of being remotely entertained by Israel, and it has long been abandoned by the Palestinian leadership.

The fifth scenario consisted of returning none of the refugees. It predicted the total collapse of the peace talks and further deterioration in the conditions of the Palestinian refugees and their rights in Arab countries. In the meantime, and in the absence of full return of the refugees, the author asked: What next? He dealt with the status of the refugees in the Arab countries on the basis of two related concepts: integration (*idmaj*) and resettlement, as understood by both Israel and the West, on the one hand, and the Arab states on the other. Whatever rights the Arab countries have granted to the refugees, such as the right to work, own property, and have access to education and health care (as for example in Syria and Iraq and to varying degrees in the Gulf countries, mainly prior to the Gulf War, and Egypt), only partial integration was implied, the assumption being that the refugees would retain their political identity and eventually return home. Jordan was the only exception in granting most of the refugees full rights.

In discussing compensation, Al-Az'ar noted only that compensation and the right of return are not mutually exclusive and that even those who are allowed to return are entitled to compensation. Their suffering over the years as refugees and the disruption of their normal existence are immeasurable in monetary terms. Israel, the author stated, is the main party that should be held accountable for paying compensation. For Israel, however, paying compensation is "the other face of resettlement." Compensation, for Israel, means accepting resettlement in lieu of return.

To strengthen the case of the refugees, alleviate their living conditions, and make sure that their rights are safeguarded (including the option to return), Al-Az'ar made a number of suggestions. Resolution of the refugee issue will take time, but short-term ways to alleviate their harsh day-to-day living conditions yet may be sought; this could be accomplished by implementing international standards of human rights regarding the protection of refugees and by harmonizing Arab state legislation toward refugees, bringing them in line with relevant international agreements. Additionally, UNRWA's work as a relief organization should be separate from recent attempts at carrying out aid programs in conjunction with the Middle East peace process, the so-called Peace

Implementation Projects (PIPs); any move toward quick liquidation of UNRWA operations that does not take into account the necessary measures needed to cope with the ensuing vacuum will definitely lead to a worsening of the conditions of the refugees. When the refugees are brought under the umbrella of international protection and in line with the declaration of the Copenhagen Conference of 1995, the host states have the right to ask for assistance in alleviating refugee conditions.

During the phasing out of UNRWA, money obtained from Israel through compensation schemes should be channeled into supporting any curtailed or phased-out UNRWA services. Close coordination should be established between Palestinian refugees in the diaspora and those remaining under the PA in a manner similar to that between Israel and the Jewish diaspora. This coordination should be entrusted to a private body other than the PA. Finally, Al-Az'ar advocated offering the Palestinians protection through dual citizenship. Palestinians everywhere ought to be canvassed, and those not wishing to return ought to be compensated and given adequate legal protection under international law.

An unusual joint Palestinian-Israeli proposal for dealing with the refugees was offered by Mark Heller and Sari Nusseibeh, authors of *No Trumpets, No Drums* (1991). As an essential ingredient of their two-state solution, the authors proposed the following with regard to the refugees:

(1) The new Palestinian state should prepare to absorb between 750,000 and 1 million returnees, most of whom are camp residents.

(2) Palestinians who choose to remain where they are should be offered "citizenship and full political rights [in their host countries], while in no way detracting from any rights or privileges that such Palestinians may enjoy in the Palestinian State" (p. 88). This Palestinian citizenship should be offered to all Palestinians, regardless of where they live, including Palestinians who are citizens of Israel.

(3) Israeli claims that the admission of close to 1 million returnees into the occupied territories may not be technically feasible should be rejected because of Israel's own plans under the Likud government at the time to settle an additional three-quarters of a million settlers in the occupied territory.

(4) Selecting a small number of returnees for admission to Israel proper should be guided by humanitarian considerations and decided on a case-by-case basis.

(5) An international body of assessors should be appointed to estimate the value of abandoned Palestinian property. Against this value, the authors suggest taking into account the cost of settling Palestinians in the occupied territories and elsewhere, and "perhaps even the value of Jewish properties in Arab countries" (p. 96).

(6) The authors link the continued future existence of Jewish settlements in the occupied territories to the return of a limited number of Palestinians to Israel. This will not be a true reciprocal arrangement, however, because the Palestinians returning to Israel will live under full Israeli jurisdiction, whereas the settlers would continue to hold Israeli citizenship and the settlements would be given a measure of municipal autonomy under Israeli jurisdiction.

(7) Jewish owners of property in the future Palestinian state, whether purchased before or after 1948, should be allowed to apply for Palestinian citizenship and live in the Palestinian state should they desire. Further Jewish acquisition of property in the future Palestinian state should not be restricted.

No survey of nonofficial Palestinian approaches would be complete without mentioning the work of Atef Kubursi, a Lebanese economist, and Sami Hadawi, a Palestinian land taxation official in the Mandatory Government of Palestine who was also employed in the early 1950s as a land-assessment expert with the UN Palestine Conciliation Commission in New York. In their book *Palestinian Rights and Losses in 1948* (1988), they defined refugee compensation in terms of reparations, restitution, and indemnification. Four different components entered their calculations of Palestinian losses in 1948: (1) immovable property, which consists of public infrastructural property, privately and collectively owned land in urban as well as rural areas; (2) movable property, which covers items such as consumer durables and means of production; (3) lost opportunities, reflected in the loss of income due to lost business, job, and educational opportunities; and (4) psychological damage related to one's "security, safety, identity, and self-realization." Deprivation of the latter "commodities" have economic consequences because they "would force individuals to lower [their] levels of utility" (p. 121).

Kubursi and Hadawi's global figure of material and nonmaterial losses amounted to nearly 1.182 billion Palestinian pounds in 1948 prices. Conversion of this figure to U.S. dollars, and its adjustment for U.S. inflation rates, yields an all-inclusive figure of $147 billion at 1984 prices. The figure is reduced to $92 billion if compensation is limited to physical property valuation (p. 183). The authors were careful not to imply that compensation must be considered in lieu of implementation of the right of return according to Resolution 194 (III). Rather, they viewed compensation as one of the options delineated by the resolution, the other being the right of return.

5 | Other Approaches to Refugees

The question of Palestine attracted the attention of scholars well before the creation of the refugee problem in 1948. However, with the start of the Middle East peace talks in the early 1990s, research into the Palestine question in general and the status of refugees in particular has received heightened interest. In response to the needs of the multilateral working groups of the Middle East peace process, several bibliographies were prepared bearing on the politics, sociology, law, and economy of the Middle East. The Center for Refugee Studies at York University in Canada published in 1992 a bibliography commissioned by the RWG, which included almost 1,000 references grouped around the six main themes of the RWG. Another annotated bibliography, edited by Andrew Watson (1994) and published by the University of Toronto, listed nearly 2,000 references of direct and indirect relevance to Palestinian refugees, and the Norwegian Institute for Applied Social Science in Oslo distributed at the December 1995 meeting of the RWG the draft of an analytic bibliography dating back to 1991 with almost 500 references on Palestinian refugees culled from Arabic, Hebrew, English, and French sources (Endresen and Zureik 1995).

The literature on Palestinian refugees is voluminous. This chapter deals with the three main themes of the study--the right of return, compensation, and resettlement--as discussed by non-Palestinian and non-Israeli writers. Its purpose is to complement the discussions presented in chapters 3 and 4, which discuss Israeli and Palestinian approaches to the refugee issues, respectively. Although the views discussed below are presented independently, the policy implications derived from them tend to support indirectly (and in some instances directly) either the Palestinian or Israeli side of the debate.

The half dozen writers discussed in this chapter fall into two groups: One addresses the right of return, compensation, and resettlement in ways familiar to the thrust of the discussion so far, and the other approaches the right of return from the perspective of self-determination.

Right of Return, Resettlement, and Compensation

One of the early and most prolific writers on issues affecting Palestinian refugees is Don Peretz, professor emeritus of political science at Binghamton State University of New York. His *Israel and the Palestine Arabs* (1958), written almost forty years ago, was a reasonably balanced study that did not shy away from critically discussing the devastating impact of Israel's policies toward the refugees during the first decade of the state. Peretz's research offered insight into CCP attempts to set up a scheme for refugee compensation, Israel's Absentee Property Law (1950) and its Development Authority (1951), and the office of the Custodian of Absentee Property, which remains to this day. It also gave preliminary estimates of the size of lost Arab land and property.

Peretz's more recent work on the subject--notably a monograph giving an overview of the Palestine refugee issue prepared for the United States Institute of Peace (1993) and a shorter study on refugee compensation for the Center for Policy Analysis on Palestine (1995)--draws on his earlier expertise. On crucial aspects of the debate, however, Peretz's conclusions regarding the right of return are not too dissimilar from those highlighted in mainstream Israeli approaches summarized above. He maintained that nowhere does Resolution 194 (III) say that refugees have a "right of return," but rather that the refugees "should be permitted" to return. The unfortunate implication is that the choice of return lies not so much with the dispossessed refugees but with those who are largely responsible for their dispersal.

Peretz also rejected the international law basis of the resolution's right of return. In his view, "international codes" stress the resettlement of refugees rather than their repatriation, and in any case, he argued, international law stipulates that the return should be to the country of which the refugee was or is a citizen. In essence, Peretz maintained that since international law is premised on state sovereignty, the "right of return" presupposes the existence of a "country" of which one is (was) a citizen and to which one can return. For Peretz (and others), this right does not apply to the Palestinian refugees; the Palestinians do not have the right of return because Israel is (was) not their state.

Peretz's 1995 study on refugee compensation acknowledged the historical dimension of Palestinian claims more forcefully but remained faithful to his notion that "while there is little dispute about the right of refugees unable or unwilling to return to their original homes to receive restitution for property left behind, this principle does not appear explicitly in international law" (1995, 1). He applied this same reasoning to the question of compensating Jewish immigrants from the Arab countries who settled in Israel. This group of immigrants, represented by WOJAC (which has official status in Israel), estimated the cost of Israel's absorption of Jewish immigrants from the Arab countries to be about $11.5 billion, an amount which, it argued, should be charged to the Arab governments; Peretz noted that this estimate of the value of Jewish property left behind in Arab countries is five times larger than that left by the Palestinian refugees. Efforts are underway in Israel to gather proof of Jewish property previously owned in Arab countries for future negotiations in a final settlement.

Peretz concluded that compensation is best handled on a collective rather than individual basis. He reached this conclusion through a slightly different route from the one adopted by other writers, arguing that it would be almost impossible to identify all the rightful owners. Land ownership records in Palestine are incomplete and in disarray; some were destroyed during the fighting in 1948, and "some of the microfilmed material sent to England was later found to be illegible, and many documents had certain basic omissions" (p. 16). In addition, most of the abandoned Arab land, amounting to close to 90 percent of the area of Palestine (23 out of 26 million dunums), was not properly registered, including most of the Arab-owned cultivable land amounting to 4,574,000 dunums. The situation was further complicated by the use in Palestine of the collective system of land ownership known as the *musha'a*, which extended to between 40 and 50 percent of the land in Palestine. Land inheritance across generations, in conjunction with the *musha'a* system, contributed to excessive fragmentation and parceling of land, which makes the task of identifying individual owners extremely difficult.

Peretz suggested that any global settlement of the refugee issue must be considered in a regional context. Aid for developing the economy of the region, he argued, must be fused with money paid for refugee compensation. He proposed setting up a refugee bank that would be in charge of distributing compensation money and making loans available with a view to encouraging the refugees to become self-sufficient through initiating income-generating projects. On the basis of UNRWA's experience in financing loans for income-generating projects, Peretz expected that the refugees would be prepared to "give up their refugee status" (p. 18). The final balance sheet resulting from any international efforts to come up with the needed money for global compensation should also include the value of Jewish property in Arab countries, value of Jewish property damaged during the war, and the price of vacated Jewish settlements in the prospective Palestinian state in the West Bank and Gaza.

Several writers (Radley 1978; Hannum 1987; Frelick 1990) argued that human rights law does not apply to the Palestinian refugees' right of return. Radley, for example, described Article 13, paragraph 12 of the Universal Declaration of Human Rights as "irrelevant to the question whether a right exists on the part of the Palestinian refugees to return to Israel," whereas Hannum noted "the general inapplicability of the right of return set forth in article 12 of the Covenant to the resolution of situations such as that of the Palestinians." Both Hannum (1987) and Mubanga-Chipoya (1988) concurred that the best way of addressing Palestinian rights is through dealing with the issue of self-determination (cited in Takkenberg 1995, 25). In Mubanga-Chipoya's words (1988), "satisfaction of the principle [of self-determination] for the Arab Palestinians will also meet the right to return" (p. 25).

A much bolder attempt at dealing with refugee claims and status is undertaken by Donna Artz, a lawyer who teaches at Syracuse University. Based on work in progress for the New York-based Council on Foreign Relations, she advocated in a recent op-ed piece for the *Jordan Times* (7 July 1995) a slight, though important, variation on the Israeli regional solution. Under an eye-catching title, "Negotiating the Last Taboo: Palestinian Refugees," Artz proposed settling most of the Palestinians in Jordan by giving them dual citizenship or at least a Palestinian identity card and providing them with compensation for property lost in 1948. Most of those in Syria, she wrote, "are virtual citizens," and that arrangement should be formalized. Between 1 and 1.5 million could be settled in the occupied territories, North Africa, and the Gulf. Finally, she argued, Israel should accept between 50,000 and 100,000 Palestinian refugees into Israel proper, as long as its neighbors are willing to accept a similar number of Palestinians for resettlement.

Howard Adelman (1993, 1988, 1985), a Canadian academic and philosopher by training, has been writing now for more than a decade on Palestinian refugees. Adelman, who has been consistently hostile to and critical of UNRWA, portrayed the organization as highly bureaucratized and self-serving, whose continued existence is due more to its "inertia" than to real needs of the refugees. Overall, Adelman contended, UNRWA has been an obstacle to resolving the refugee issue. It has created a highly dependent constituency from among the Palestinian refugee community, which is better served by having UNRWA dismantled and its aid channeled to the refugees directly so as to contribute to their economic self-sufficiency and eventual integration in the host societies.

Adelman's echoing of the Israeli approach to the refugee problem is equally evident in his insistence that UN Resolution 194(III) and other international instruments bearing on refugee rights do not translate into binding laws granting the Palestinians the right to return to their 1948 territory, let alone to their original homes. Thus, Adelman construed the right of return to mean the right to return to a "homeland" and argued that this homeland is the West Bank and Gaza.

Although these writers do not reflect consensus on the refugee issue, they clearly have a great deal in common among themselves and with the Israeli writers discussed in chapter 3. In contrast, the views presented below approach the refugee issue from international law and human rights perspectives, with the right to self determination being a cornerstone (Takkenberg 1995; Cassese 1993; UN 1978, 1979).

Self-Determination and the Right of Return

The United Nations Committee on the Exercise of the Inalienable Rights of the Palestinian People commissioned two studies with direct bearing on the issues at hand. *The Right of Return of the Palestinian People* (1978) and *The Right of Self-Determination of the Palestinian People* (1979) establish a link between individual right (which is the basis of the right of return) and collective right of return as it applied to a dispossessed national group. Refugee right of return, first enunciated in 1946 by the Economic and Social Council of the United Nations, was reaffirmed in the Council's 1973 draft principle, which states:

a) Everyone is entitled, without distinction of any kind, such as race, color, sex, language, religion, political or other opinion, national or social origin, property, marriage or other social status, to return to his country. (b) No one shall be arbitrarily deprived of his nationality or forced to renounce his nationality as a means of divesting him of the right to return to his country. (c) No one shall be arbitrarily deprived of the right to return to his own country. (d) No one should be denied the right to return to his own country on the ground that he has no passport or other travel documents. (cited in UN 1978, 6)

The right of return, which is stipulated in Resolution 194 (III), is also affirmed in the Universal Declaration of Human Rights of 1948, a cornerstone of international law. Article 13 states that "1. Everyone has a right to freedom of movement and residence within boundaries of each state. 2. Everyone has the right to leave any country, including his own, and to return to his country." More importantly, it should be noted that in 1974 the Palestinian right of return was linked, through General Assembly Resolution 3236 (XXIX), to their right of self-determination. What is significant about this resolution, as rightly pointed out by Tadmor (1994), is that it does not distinguish between the 1948 and 1967 refugees. It addresses Palestinian refugees' right of return as one group. The resolution states:

> 1. Reaffirming the inalienable right of the Palestinian people in Palestine, including: (a) The right to self-determination without external interference; (b) the right to national independence and sovereignty;
> 2. Reaffirms also the inalienable right of the Palestinians to return to their homes and property from which they have been displaced and uprooted, and calls for their return. (UN 1979, 34)

Antonio Cassese, a renowned international jurist, overcame the shortcoming of Security Council Resolution 242 of 22 November 1967, which sidesteps the issue of right of return, not to mention self-determination. According to Cassese (1993), the 1974 General Assembly Resolution 3236 (XXIX) is crucial, because it moved the debate from the "individual's 'right of return' to the Palestinian people's right for self-determination" (p. 12). Moreover, in place of the phrase "Palestinian refugees," the Resolution now refers to the "Palestinian people." Cassese dealt with two likely objections to holding a plebiscite in order to ascertain, in the words of the International Court of Justice, whether the choice for self-determination reflects "the free and genuine expression of the peoples concerned" (p. 13). First, it could be objected that self-determination is contingent on sovereignty and (similar to the argument against the right of return) that self-determination cannot be exercised in this case because the West Bank and Gaza were not and have not been sovereign territories. "The response to this objection," wrote Cassese, "is that self-determination is not contingent on sovereignty; it is a concept geared to peoples, not to sovereign titles" (p. 13). Objections to self-determination may rely on a second familiar claim that the status of the territories has been altered due to the building of Jewish settlements in the area, which basically altered the population composition; however, Cassese rejected this objection as well "by noting that those settlements are illegal as being contrary to international norms on belligerent occupation" and that "Israeli settlers should not be permitted to take part in a possible referendum or plebiscite" (p. 13). However, he concluded by noting that in as much as the weight of international law and its moral force are compelling in favor of Palestinian rights, his suggestion remains "unworkable--unless it becomes part of a 'package deal' agreed upon by all the parties concerned" (p. 13). It remains to be seen whether the DOP, Oslo II, or the final status agreements are able to translate Palestinian rights into an expression of self-determination through statehood. So far, Israeli interpretations have insisted on autonomy devoid of legal independence and statehood. This is particularly true with regard to the Likud's position.

Takkenberg's (1995) patient and thorough analysis of international law as applied to the Palestinian situation has resulted in the following series of observations: (1) the right of return in general derives its legitimacy from customary international law, according to which "[f]or most individuals the actual practice of returning to one's home or country is so commonplace a part of everyday living that the right of return as a legal concept is given little attention" (Mallison and Mallison 1979, cited in Takkenberg 1995, 5); (2) the four Geneva Conventions of 1949 stipulate repatriation of war victims, whether civilians or military personnel; (3) of the "three durable" solutions advocated by UNHCR for solving the refugee problem--voluntary repatriation, integration in host countries, and resettlement in third countries--the first is singled out as the best solution; and (4) when refugee exodus was prompted by expulsion, as occurred with the Palestinians, "the right of return infers from the illegality of the expulsion itself. It is generally recognized that a state cannot legally expel a population under its control. Those expelled clearly have the right to reverse an illegal act, that is, to return to their homeland" (Takkenberg 1995, 7).

Takkenberg disagreed with the restricted interpretations regarding the inapplicability of the law of return to the Palestinian situation. Like Artz and Zughaib (1993), he found the law of return relevant when interpreted to mean the return to one's own country or homeland. The right of return could thus be exercised in Palestine if not Israel. In other words, the right of return as a *principle* remains operable, although its territorial exercise would have to be defined. This raises the same question posed earlier: "What or where is Palestine?"

According to Cassese, Takkenberg, and others, the DOP of September 1993 has opened the way for subsuming the right of return under that of self-determination. Following mutual recognition, the PLO has been in a position to negotiate with Israel as the representative of the Palestinian people and has recognized Israel's right to exist. As the UN study (1979) *The Right of Self-Determination of the Palestinian People* pointed out, the response to Security Council Resolution 242 of 1967, which mentions in general terms "the refugee problem," was a succession of UN General Assembly resolutions that referred to the "inalienable rights of the Palestinian people" and that reaffirmed Palestinian rights as an "indispensable element in the establishment of a just and lasting peace in the Middle East" (1969 UNGA Resolution 2535-B[XXIV], 1970 UNGA Resolution 2672-C[XXV], cited in UN 1979, 33). The passage of the crucial General Assembly Resolution 3236(XXIX) on 22 November 1974 for the first time reaffirmed the inalienable rights of the Palestinian people in Palestine in terms of self-determination and the return of the refugees to their homes.

When attempts were made in 1976 to proceed with a similar resolution to the Security Council, the United States blocked adoption of the resolution. What was brought back into the DOP from the UN arsenal of resolutions on Palestine were Security Council Resolutions 242 and 338, neither of which addresses the issue of return, let alone self-determination.

Under Israel's insistence, most of the activity pertaining to refugee return has been handled so far under family reunification, yet very little academic research has addressed the topic. Exceptions to this are the contributions by Quigley (1992) and Zedalis (1992). Both addressed the right of return to the 1967 occupied Palestinian lands. Quigley argued that there are four categories of refugees resulting from the 1967 war: those who were driven out by the Israelis during the fighting as confirmed by various United Nations and independent reports; those who happened to be outside the territories (studying, working, visiting) when the 1967 war broke out and were not allowed to return; those who left after 1967 to study, work, or live abroad temporarily and were not allowed back after their residency permits had expired; and those expelled by Israel on so-called security grounds. Only minute numbers in any of these categories have been allowed back by Israel. Israel's response has been threefold: first, to argue that those who left/were expelled in 1967 would not be allowed to return until the issue of borders is settled between Israel and her neighbors and that most of these refugees left voluntarily; second, that any returnees allowed to return would be admitted on a humanitarian, case-by-case basis; and third, that security considerations prevent Israel from allowing the return of the refugees. There is a familiar ring to these reasons: They are similar to those given by Israel in justifying its refusal to allow the return of the 1948 refugees.

Quigley based his right-of-return argument on familiar grounds: humanitarian law (as per the Hague Regulations and the Geneva Convention), human rights law (the Universal Declaration of Human Rights, Convention on the Rights of the Child, Convention on the Nationality of Married Women, and the Helsinki Family Act), UN Security Council Resolution 237, and international law (International Convention on the Protection of the Rights of All Migrant Workers and Members of their Families). Humanitarian law is intended to deal with families separated by hostilities, but it does not deal with families who live under belligerent occupation where the split occurred after the occupation had taken place. Here Quigley relied on human rights instruments. He cited examples from several countries, including Israel within the Green Line, which show that family reunification is guaranteed to spouses and children, whether or not the applicant is a citizen of the intended country of residence. Quigley concluded his essay by noting that "[h]uman personal association is one of the most basic of rights. Individuals must be free to marry and establish a family with others of their own choosing. States may not interfere with that right by holding one spouse or child on the other side of the border. Israel's violation of these rights is a reminder of their importance and of the need for a more effective system for the international implementation of rights" (p. 251).

Israel has consistently refused to apply human rights law (the Universal Declaration, Covenant on Civil and Political Rights, and Geneva Convention) or international law (the Geneva Civilians Convention of 1949) aimed at the return of the Palestinians (even though it is bound by these agreements). Zedalis (1992) argued that "Israel's refusal serves to modify its international legal obligations" (p. 515) and suggested that in these circumstances where "persistent objections free one from customary standards, and bona fide reservation works the same effect on standards of conventional sort," the right of the Palestinians to return "must rest exclusively on Article 49 of the Civilians Convention. If it is not, then human rights law must be invoked" (p. 516).

6 | Conclusions and Implications

As I write this final chapter in the spring of 1996, the situation on the ground in the West Bank and Gaza (not to mention Lebanon) has deteriorated significantly compared to a year ago, with the Palestinian population having turned its anger onto the PA and progress toward peace between Israel and the Palestinians remaining in limbo. Demonstrations by Palestinians against the PA have become frequent, at times resembling past scenes of confrontation and protest against Israeli occupation. It is not far-fetched to assume that this trend (if it continues) will fuel an internal crisis among the Palestinians and will further weaken the PA in its negotiations with Israel. There seems to be a feeling that the PA's concessions to Israel have resulted in a situation where the Palestinian enclaves in the West Bank and Gaza that grew out of Oslo II are being treated as colonies subject to unilateral Israeli decisions. Closures, curfews, sea blockade, mass arrests, and demolitions of Palestinian homes--vintage Israeli actions dating back to the days of the intifada--are once again becoming a regular Israeli staple in dealing with the Palestinian population. Improvements can hardly be expected under the new Likud government.

Palestinians fear that the issues of water, borders, Jerusalem, settlements, and refugees to be addressed in the final status talks will end on an already large heap of concessions made by the Palestinians to the Israelis in the two major agreements concluded so far: Oslo I and Oslo II. Given the Clinton administration's desire to go into the November 1996 American elections with some tangible results to show from Palestinian-Israeli talks, it will likely do its utmost to ensure that the peace process does not collapse or at least that it maintains the *appearance* of being alive. However, unless the situation on the ground improves for Palestinians (and for Israelis, though for different reasons), there are those who believe that a breakdown in the talks may be preferable to their continuation as envisaged by the Israelis.

Despite the negative signals of recent months, I proceed on the assumption that the peace talks will continue in one form or another, even if in a delayed, erratic fashion. The following issues will have relevance to the final status talks on refugees: future Palestinian population and refugee distribution; the right of return; family reunification; compensation; status of Palestinians in Arab countries; attitudes of refugees; and the future of UNRWA.

Population

The foregoing analysis has shown that under a worst-case scenario-- i.e., a modest number of Palestinians returning to the West Bank and Gaza and an almost negligible number of the 1948 refugees returning to Israel--the current Arab-Jewish population balance in historic Palestine will remain in Israel's favor in the short term. Within slightly more than a decade, the gap will close, and the estimated population of 10 million will be almost evenly split in Mandatory Palestine. In addition, slightly more than 5 million Palestinians will continue to reside in the diaspora, mainly Jordan, Syria, and Lebanon, thus bringing the total number of Palestinians worldwide to at least 10 million in a decade. In other words, despite the various attempts to reduce the Palestinian presence in Palestine, including the expulsion and exodus of the 1948 war and the displacement of the 1967 war, and despite the obstructionist measures adopted by Israel on the refugee issue during the Middle East peace talks, a significant number of Palestinians will remain in their ancestral homes and are likely to become a majority in two decades, all things being equal.

My estimate is that there are currently close to 4 million Palestinian refugees and displaced persons, more than two-thirds of whom continue to reside outside historical Palestine. To the extent that Israel will allow the return of displaced people and refugees to the West Bank and Gaza, the numbers will be small, as we have seen in this study. Israel will invoke security considerations, absorptive capacity of the territories, and economic constraints to argue against admission of large numbers. However, the establishment of a Palestinian state in the West Bank and Gaza, and the likely introduction of a Palestinian law of return, if carried out judiciously, will further accelerate the crystallization of a stable Palestinian presence in historic Palestine.

For this to happen, several things must take place. Assuming the eventual creation of a Palestinian state, a proper absorption ministry must be set up to plan the phased return of the 1967 displaced persons and the 1948 refugees and address their needs. Issues of housing, employment, education, and health, among others, must be tackled in a sober and systematic fashion. Thus, the evidence suggests that housing, unemployment, and matching the skills of returnees with labor market requirements may be some of the major adjustment problems facing the returnees.

Palestinian reliance on the Israeli labor market must be minimized in the future with a view to accomplishing two objectives. There is a need to develop Palestinian human resources and to gear them to nation building. This will not happen if Palestinian livelihood in the future Palestinian state continues to be dependent, as it is now, on the Israeli metropolis and its labor market--in which the Palestinians continue to be the hewers of wood and drawers of water for the Israeli economy. Severing the economic dependency on Israel will in the long run reverse Palestinian underdevelopment caused largely by systematic Israeli policies of exploitation and deprivation during more than a quarter of a century of occupation. These moves should be accompanied by proper use of natural resources, in particular land reclamation and revival of the agricultural sector, which all but perished under Israeli occupation. Above all, the proper use of human resources must be carried out to benefit both the future state and its Palestinian citizens--those who are already there and those who will be joining it. In this context, it is worth pointing out that, unless concrete plans are put in place to this effect, the new state is unlikely to attract highly skilled expatriate Palestinian manpower. Furthermore, in the face of continued violation of basic democratic principles by the PA and the absence of political stability, hopes once attached to Palestinian and other capital finding its way into investment projects will prove vain.

A concerted effort should be directed toward building the much-needed infrastructure to enhance the absorptive capacity of the West Bank and Gaza: roads, housing, telecommunications systems, schools, hospitals, and other infrastructure aspects of nation building. No less than fifty studies on infrastructure requirements have been carried out by private international organizations, UN agencies, the World Bank, the International Monetary Fund, and Palestinian researchers.

Special job and vocational training and counselling programs should be put in place, for both returnees and those who are already in the West Bank and Gaza. The evidence so far is that, except for the police, the majority of the returnees are unable to find jobs or are unqualified for the jobs available (Zureik 1996). The returnees should be counselled and eventually trained for the kinds of jobs that are available or that will soon be in demand. This training must be an integral part of the returnees' adaptation program, if repatriation is to succeed.

It is unlikely that the average returnee will have the financial resources necessary to start a business or build a home. The setting up of a small loan program at low interest rates is one way to attract qualified Palestinians to return and may encourage those who are already there to embark on business activities.

Right of Return

In accordance with the DOP, the fate of the 1948 refugees is to be dealt with in the final status negotiations that officially opened in May 1996. Chapters 3 and 5 have demonstrated that both official and nonofficial Israeli and pro-Israeli approaches to this question have tried to raise law-based doubts regarding the binding nature of UN resolutions on the Palestinians' collective right of return. It is distressing to note that this stance is also increasingly becoming the official American one.

It should be noted that this approach flies in the face of the interpretation of General Assembly Resolution 194 (III) advanced by the CCP, which was originally established by the same resolution to "facilitate the repatriation, resettlement and economic and social rehabilitation of the refugees and the payment of compensation." For its part, the CCP offered the following authoritative interpretation of Resolution 194 (III):

> The General Assembly had laid down the principle of the right of the refugees to exercise a free choice between returning to their homes and being compensated for the loss of or damage to their property on the one hand, or, on the other, of not returning to their homes and being adequately compensated for the value of property abandoned by them. (cited in UN 1978, 15)

Nothing that I have read or seen so far leads me to believe that Israel will allow the return of any Palestinian refugees from 1948 to Israel proper. Rumors have circulated that under certain conditions Israel may allow the return of between 50,000 and 75,000 refugees for symbolic reasons to placate international public opinion. Although such figures represent a minuscule percentage of the close to 3.2 million Palestine refugees registered with UNRWA, Israel is unlikely to agree. Allowing the return of even a token number of refugees is construed by Israel as an admission of guilt regarding their exodus in 1948, for which it officially denies any responsibility.

Some analysts, notably Shlomo Gazit, suggested that Israel should make a final gesture for ending its century-long conflict with the Palestinians by issuing a statement or being party to an international body, such as the UN General Assembly, which would pass a resolution to replace Resolution 194 (III). Such a resolution would acknowledge the suffering of the Palestine refugees without making any statement of culpability. The intent behind this proposal would be to address the psychological and moral aspects of the refugee issue, short of confirming any Israeli responsibility for the 1948 Palestine refugee exodus.

Whereas the Palestinian right of return remains the cornerstone of Palestinian and Arab approaches to the refugee issue (see chapter 4), a significant shift in the articulation of the Palestinian position has taken place in the last decade, from rejection of anything short of application of Resolution 194 (III) to acceptance of other modalities. However, the Arab side operates under a major weakness of the Madrid peace formula of 1991, which was lifted from the 1978 Camp David Accords: The Madrid conference was not officially held under UN auspices and the preamble to the Madrid declaration mentioned UN Resolutions 242 and 338, and not the crucial UN Resolution 194 (III), as the basis for the Middle East peace talks.

In succumbing to the dictates of the Madrid conference, Palestinians have been framing the debate, implicitly if not explicitly, over the issue of the right of return *not* as one of whether the refugees should return to their 1948 homes, but rather as a debate over (1) whether there should be unhampered right of return for all refugees and displaced Palestinians to an independent state in the West Bank and Gaza; (2) how to compensate the refugees and normalize the civil and human rights of nonreturnees in neighboring countries; (3) whether to grant Palestinian passports to all refugees remaining in their places of refuge; and (4) how to get Israel to allow a symbolic return of some refugees from the 1948 war to Israel proper and to recognize that a historical injustice was done to the Palestinian people.

If the recent report by Ze'ev Schiff that was published in the Israeli daily *Ha-Aretz* on 22 February 1996 about secret talks taking place between the PA representatives and the Peres government is true, Israel would have assisted in the resettlement of refugees outside its borders. The only concession the Labor government would have made to the 1948 refugees would have been to agree to a small number of family reunifications on a case-by-case basis. The other item relating to the refugee issue was that Palestinians would continue to call for the right of return but that Israel would not be bound by it. This item was in line with the Labor party's platform calling for "no recognition of Palestinian right of return."

In fact, the absorption of appreciable numbers of returnees to a future Palestinian state would be severely constrained by lack of space. The West Bank and Gaza constitute less than one-quarter of the area of Mandatory Palestine. With Gaza showing the highest population density anywhere in the world, the West Bank remains the only realistic place in which to absorb returnees. A look at the territorial division of the West Bank into three zones, according to the Oslo II agreement, reveals the following:

• ZONE A, which includes Arab cities, will be under Palestinian control.

• ZONE B, over which Israel will be in charge in terms of security but will gradually hand over authority after redeployment of its forces to the elected Palestinian Council, consists of Palestinian villages.

• ZONE C, comprised of military areas, settlements, roads and state lands, will remain under Israeli control until final-status negotiations begin, with a view to transferring authority over the zone to the Palestinians by May 1999 ("Israeli-Palestinian Interim Agreement" 1996).

According to press coverage of the details of this agreement as summarized by Chomsky (1996), Zone C covers 70 percent of the West Bank, Zone A between 1 and 5 percent, and Zone B the rest. Some 1.1 million Palestinians live in Zones A and B, whereas Zone C includes 140,000 Jewish settlers; an additional 150,000 live in areas classified by Israel as part of the Jerusalem municipality but which were part of the West Bank before 1967. Unless Israel yields during the final status talks on settlements and vacates Zone C, it is difficult to see how it would be possible to accommodate a significant number of Palestinian returnees.

The fate of the close to 150,000 Palestinian refugees from 1948 who live inside Israel proper, but who have been prevented from returning to their villages for nearly half a century, is not part of the negotiations over refugees. They amount to close to 20 percent of the Palestinian population in Israel proper. Being citizens of Israel has in a sense closed the doors before them in terms of appealing their case to a neutral, international adjudicating body and disadvantaged their claim to return to their homes. From the point of view of international and humanitarian law, they are the truly displaced and have an uncontested right to return to their homes; however, Israel contends that they are free to present their grievances to the courts in Israel, which they have done consistently, to no avail. When the courts recommended the return of some, the implementation of the order was frozen by the government.

In all its bilateral discussions with Israel, the PLO has shied away from even mentioning the internal refugees for fear of jeopardizing other, more pressing concerns as defined by the PLO, such as further withdrawal by Israel from the Palestinian areas and the culmination of a Palestinian state.

Family Reunification

It is clear that in the initial phase, and until the Palestinian state becomes a reality, the return to the West Bank and Gaza will be guided by family reunification criteria. It is necessary to approach family reunification not as a privilege subject to myriad political and administrative criteria (the current approach), but as a right. Human rights law, for example, stresses the integrity of the unity of the family, and this should be brought to bear in the case of Palestinian repatriations.

Ensuring the unity of the family is not only based on a legal conception of such a right, which most countries enshrine in their immigration legislation, but it also has practical consequences. Inability of family members across state boundaries to draw on the psychological and social support of other family members exacerbates the personal and familial problems encountered by the returnees and makes the process of adaptation all the more difficult.

The criteria and decisions regarding family reunification must be made more transparent and accountable. Some of this is being accomplished (at least on paper) as a result of the ongoing discussions in the Quadripartite Committee involving Palestinians, Israelis, Jordanians, and

Egyptians; however, some returnees interviewed by the author (Zureik 1996) felt that *wasta* (commissions paid to middlemen) and other nonuniversalistic or political criteria sometimes play an inordinate role in determining who is given a residency permit. Standardization and simplification of such procedures will lessen the monetary and social costs involved.

Compensation

With regard to compensation, the debate revolves around determining the number of people who should receive it, how to calculate the amount, how to administer it, and the source of the money. I do not think Israel is likely to make an issue about the numbers of refugees, once the discussion is confined to resettlement and compensation. As noted above, Israel is likely to stress material, collective forms of compensation and to reject compensation that is based on the true value of individual losses and takes into account nonmaterial losses, i.e., indemnification. It will also insist on setting up an international monitoring body that will contribute to the fund, share in its administration, and ensure accountability. Israel will also insist that UNRWA be dismantled and that part of the compensation should be directed to revive the economies of the region.

The Arab side should present a maximal case for compensation, by stressing that it should be based on a calculation of individual losses, that each refugee claimant is entitled to receive the true value of losses incurred at current prices, and that these losses should reflect both material and nonmaterial losses. Serious attempts should be made to consult the CCP archives, the British and Arab records, and the refugees themselves to establish the magnitude of Palestinian losses in 1948. On the basis of this approach, preliminary estimates of the value of Palestinian lost property, movable and immovable, plus the cost of lost career opportunities and psychological damage incurred, come to about $147 billion in 1984 prices, compared to $92 billion if confined to material losses only. This is compared to a meager sum of $2 billion mentioned by Israeli researchers, where the frame of reference is the money pledged under the umbrella of the RWG.

It is worth noting in this regard that when Israeli settlers were evicted from the Sinai in the wake of the Camp David agreement between Israel and Egypt, each settler household was compensated $250,000, yet Israeli researchers refer to a compensation package of $10,000-20,000 per refugee household, and some Palestinian researchers suggest $20,000 per refugee.

In host countries where Palestinian refugees have been granted citizenship status, such as Jordan, which has diplomatic relations with Israel, the host government will in all likelihood press for individual compensation for its citizens of Palestinian refugee origin. It is important, therefore, that Palestinian negotiators coordinate their strategy on this score, not only with Jordan, but ultimately with all Arab states that have significant Palestinian communities.

In addition to the losses caused by the 1948 and 1967 wars, the Palestinians are entitled to submit claims for property damage and personal indemnification as a result of Israel's conduct during its occupation of the West Bank and Gaza. Individual Palestinians have already initiated court action against Israel for damage caused by its forces during the intifada. The suggestion by members of the Israeli government so far has been to deal with such claims in a collective fashion and to prevent individual cases from ever reaching the courts.

The issue of Jewish losses in Arab countries is raised by Israeli and other writers and no doubt will be officially raised by Israel. The Palestinian position on compensation of Jewish losses in Arab countries was made clear by the head of the Palestinian delegation to the second RWG meeting in Ottawa (1992), who argued at the time that the relevant Arab governments, and not the Palestinian refugees, should bear responsibility for compensating Jewish immigrants from Arab countries.

Status of Refugees in Arab Countries

The position of Arab governments with regard to possible solutions to the refugee problem is unclear, with the exception of Jordan and Lebanon. When the time comes, Arab governments that have hosted large numbers of refugees for nearly half a century undoubtedly will submit their own bills. In a recent paper based on the official Jordanian position, it was estimated that Jordan contributed around $300 million annually from its own budget to the refugees in Jordan (Jaber 1996).

The Lebanese have been the most vocal concerning the presence of Palestinian refugees in their midst. Practically all observers, including Israelis, have singled out the Palestinians in Lebanon as the most vulnerable group of Palestinian refugees. The attitude of the Lebanese government was spelled out in a series of statements made by high-level

Lebanese officials. The gist of the Lebanese position is that Palestinian refugees must be fully repatriated, if not to their original homes or to a Palestinian state, then to third countries.

The most generous stance being mentioned in this regard would be to grant the Palestinians in Lebanon limited and specific civil and social rights, as long as they held Palestinian citizenship accorded to them by a Palestinian state in the West Bank and Gaza. Under this proposal, Palestinians would not be allowed to vote, run for political office, or hold public sector jobs. They would also not be allowed to invest in sectors of the economy that have a direct bearing on national security, nor would they be allowed to own communications media. They would be permitted to seek employment opportunities and enjoy freedom of movement, as long as reciprocal arrangements were made with the Palestinian state, meaning that Lebanese nationals could enjoy similar rights in areas under Palestinian jurisdiction.

Once Syria reaches an agreement with Israel over the Golan Heights, the issue of Palestinian refugees in Syria would be resolved by giving them the option to return and live in the Palestinian state or to receive Syrian citizenship. For all intents and purposes, the Palestinians in Syria are treated on an equal footing with Syrian citizens and all that is needed, once an agreement is reached between Israel and Syria, is to formalize their status by giving them citizenship and political rights.

The Palestinians should seek from the Arab governments a harmonization of their citizenship and immigration laws with international conventions and protocols bearing on refugee protection. Until the modalities for refugee settlement are worked out, international protection in the areas of human and political rights must be guaranteed. Current Arab League regulations prohibiting dual Arab nationality must be re-examined in the light of international refugee law. It would be most unfortunate, and a sure recipe for future conflict, if the current exclusionary measures against Palestinians in various Arab countries remain in effect, thus creating ghettoized Palestinian communities.

Refugee Attitudes

Although no systematic studies of refugees' views regarding possible solutions are available, a series of small-scale surveys reflects the regional variations described in chapter 2. In Lebanon, for example, Palestinian refugees' first preference is to return to their homes. Failing this, many would like to stay in Lebanon as long as their rights are normalized and they are protected through the issuance of Palestinian identity cards. Most of the Palestinians in Lebanon came from the Galilee, and so very few expressed the desire to settle in the West Bank or Gaza.

In contrast, a majority of the Palestinians in Jordan expressed an interest in having closer links with the West Bank or even returning to the West Bank. This desire is guided by matters of "principle," not by any hostility to Jordan. This finding is confirmed in another Jordanian survey in which 95 percent of camp refugees believed that Jordanian-Palestinian relations are good, and a similar proportion endorsed closer relations between Jordan and a future Palestinian state. Jordan, which accords most Palestinian refugees full citizenship, is primarily concerned with facilitating the return of the 1967 displaced people, whose fate is being discussed by the Quadripartite Committee.

A small survey of forty-two families who have returned to the West Bank showed a gap between the returnees' expectations and the reality they faced (Zureik 1996). It did not make a difference whether the returnee had previously lived in or was familiar with the new environment. Feelings of disappointment concerning politics, economy, housing, and society in general were voiced by many who returned. Although these were not sufficient reasons to compel them to abandon their plans to return home, the continuation of unfavorable political and economic conditions could very well deter others from returning and make the whole process of refugee return and family reunification a bitter and protracted experience.

UNRWA

Since its inception in 1949, UNRWA has received both criticism and praise from various quarters (e.g., Viorst 1989). Palestinians praise UNRWA for providing much-needed services to the refugees, but they also have accused the organization of acting to liquidate their cause by providing education but not employment opportunities, thus contributing to the emigration of talented youth from the occupied territories in search of work elsewhere (Elnajjar 1993). On the other hand, Israel and even some Arab governments have accused UNRWA of nourishing a politicized environment in the camps, which became a breeding ground for political and military activism (Schiff 1989).

When UNRWA's comprehensive history is finally written (see B. Schiff 1995), there is no doubt that this unique organization, which has been vilified by many, will emerge as crucial in contributing to the survival of Palestinian identity in exile. Its schools and health-care system, which cater to more than 3 million registered refugees, must be credited with keeping illiteracy in check and fending off epidemics. Moreover, UNRWA has employed more than 20,000 Palestinian administrators, managers, teachers, nurses, and doctors, thus building a formidable structure for developing human resources. The rush to move UNRWA's headquarters from Vienna to Gaza in July 1996, and eventually to close its operations down within four years, may symbolically signify that the refugee problem has been solved. This may prove to be more wishful thinking than reality.

To expect the PA to carry out the task of nation building alone, with its limited resources, and without UNRWA, is to expect the impossible. At this stage, and for the coming few years, the PA is hardly capable of catering to the refugees' needs in the West Bank and Gaza, let alone in neighboring countries. UNRWA's operations must be phased out gradually, in order to ensure the orderly transfer of functions. Equally important, a task force should be set up in order to transfer to the PA the wealth of knowledge gained by UNRWA over almost half a century of service in the areas of health, education, vocational training, and management. A technical task force should be set up to preserve UNRWA's mammoth and unique archives, which chronicle in detail the history of Palestinian dispersal since 1948.

Postscript

The narrow election victory of Benjamin Netanyahu in May 1996 sent the Arab states, including the Palestinians, and the Americans, who staked so much on a Peres victory, scurrying for clues to the Likud's plans for the peace process. Netanyahu and his colleagues in the Likud party had already given ample evidence in their election platform of what is in store for the peace process in general and the Palestinians in particular. The Likud platform stressed Israeli sovereignty over the whole of Jerusalem, rejected the establishment of a Palestinian state, and promised to expand Jewish settlement in the territories and to maintain control of water resources, defense and foreign affairs. The platform envisaged some form of autonomy for the Palestinians in their daily lives and closer discussion with Jordan once final status negotiations with the Palestinians get underway. Conspicuously absent was any direct mention of the refugees (Likud Platform 1996).

After Netanyahu's election, his office released a statement on 17 June outlining his government's guidelines with regard to the peace process. The statement repeated the three "no's" (no to withdrawal from the territories, no to a Palestinian state, and no to an official Palestinian presence in Jerusalem) and added a fourth one: no to the refugees' right of return "to any part of the Land of Israel west of the Jordan River" (Guidelines, 17 June 1996). In the eyes of many observers, the peace process was dealt another blow when Netanyahu appointed to his government Raphael Eitan and Ariel Sharon, who distinguished themselves in the past by demonizing the Palestinians.

Although Likud policy will differ dramatically from Labor's on a number of issues, the issue of refugees will not be one of them. From the Palestinian point of view, the performance of Labor over the refugee issue in various bilateral and multilateral fora connected with the Middle East peace talks has been disappointing. Whether it is family reunification or the return of the displaced from 1967, Israel has yielded very little and has succeeded for the last four years in obfuscating the issues and keeping the discussion in a holding pattern without accomplishing anything tangible. The Likud's signal about its position on the refugee issue came during an intersessional meeting of the RWG held in Oslo in June 1996 to discuss the database theme that Norway shepherds. At the meeting, and for the first time, the Israeli delegation dismissed as unacceptable any mention of the returnees or displaced, let alone refugees, in the final statement of the conference. As a result, and for the first time in such meetings, no final statement was issued.

If there is any difference between Labor and Likud on the refugee problem, it will be minor in nature and mainly a matter of style and not substance. Under Labor, Israel would possibly have allowed more returnees to trickle back to the West Bank over a long, protracted period. The position of the two parties will be similar with regard to the 1948 refugees. In general, however, Likud will adopt a more public, uncompromising posture with regard to the refugees and displaced persons by shrouding the discourse with arguments over security and even "terrorism," whereas Labor would have achieved a not-too-dissimilar outcome by dragging the discussion endlessly and burying any prospects for resolving the refugee issue in committee meetings and bureaucratic procedures at the bilateral and multilateral levels.

References

Abdul Shafi, Haider. 1991. Address delivered at the Madrid Peace Conference, 31 October (Available on the internet through http://www. israel-mfa.gov.il).

Abu-Lughod, Janet. 1971. "The Demographic Transformation of Palestine." In *Transformation of Palestine*, edited by Ibrahim Abu-Lughod. Evanston, IL: Northwestern University Press.

Abu Samra, Muhammad. 1992. "The Issue of the Refugees in 1948-1949." *International Problems, Society and Politics* 31, no. 1: 50-64 [Hebrew].

Abu Zayyad, Ziad. 1994. "The Palestinian Right of Return: A Realistic Approach." *Palestine-Israel Journal of Politics, Economics, and Culture* 2: 274-78.

Adelman, Howard. 1985. "Palestinian Refugees and the Peace Process." In *Peacemaking in the Middle East: Problems and Prospects*, edited by Paul Marantz and Janice Gross Stein. London: Croom Helm.

____. 1988. "Palestinian Refugees, Economic Integration and Durable Solutions." In *Refugees in the Age of Total War*, edited by Michael R. Marrus and Anna C. Bramwell. London: Unwin Hyman.

____. 1992. Review of "Reaching for the Olive Branch: UNRWA and Peace in the Middle East," by Milton Viorst. *Middle East Focus* 14, no. 2: 11-15.

______. 1993. *Refugees, the Right of Return and the Peace Process*. Paper presented at a conference on the Economics of Peace in the Middle East at Yarmouk University, Yarmouk, Jordan.

Adlakha, Arjun, Kevin L. Kinsella, and Marwan Khawajah. 1995. *Demography and the Palestinian Population with Special Emphasis on the Occupied Palestinian Territory*. Paper presented at the Population Association of America Meetings, 5-8 April, in San Francisco.

Ahmed, Hisham H., and Mary A. Williams-Ahmed. 1993. "The Impact of the Gulf Crisis on Jordan's Economic Infrastructure: A Study of the Responses of 207 Displaced Palestinian and Jordanian Workers." *Arab Studies Quarterly* 15, no. 4: 33-62.

Al-Aza'r, Khalid Muhammed. 1995. *Guarantees of Refugee Rights and Current Political Settlement*. Mimeographed [Arabic].

Al-Haj, Majid. 1986. "Adjustment Patterns of the Arab Internal Refugees in Israel." *Internal Migration* 24, no. 3: 651-73.

______. 1988. "The Arab Internal Refugees: The Emergence of a Minority Within the Minorities." *Immigrants and Minorities* 7, no. 2: 149-65.

Al-Hasan, Bilal. 1996. "Palestinian Refugees." *Majallat al-Dirasat al-Filastiniyah*, no. 26: 50-71 [Arabic].

Al-Maliki, Majdi. 1994. *Some Social Consequences of the Intifada for the Jalazoun (Refugee) Camp. Woman, Marriage and the Family*. Ramallah: Beissan Center for Research and Development [Arabic].

Al-Zaru, Nawaf. 1991. "Israeli Plans to Liquidate the Palestinian Camps." *Samed Al-Iqtisadi*, no. 83: 134-42 [Arabic].

'Amro, Tayseer. 1995. "Displaced Persons: Categories and Numbers Used by the Palestinian Delegation [to the Quadripartite Committee] (not including spouses and descendants)." *Article 74*, no. 14. Jerusalem: Alternative Information Center for Palestinian Residency and Refugee Rights.

Anderson, Benedict. 1994. *Imagined Communities*. London and New York: Verso Press.

Aner, Nadav. 1984. *Will They be Refugees Forever? Description of Conditions and Suggestions for a Solution*. Jerusalem: Israel Information Office [Hebrew].

Arian, Asher. 1995. *The Peace Process and Terror: Conflicting Trends in Israeli Public Opinion in 1995*. Tel-Aviv: Jaffee Center for Strategic Studies, Tel-Aviv University.

Artz, Donna. 1995. "Negotiating the Last Taboo: Palestinian Refugees." *Jordan Times*, 7 July.

____. 1996. *Bibliographical Essay [on Palestinian Refugees]*. Electronic mail, 24 February.

Artz, Donna, and Karen Zughaib. 1993. "Return to the Negotiated Lands: The Likelihood and Legality of a Population Transfer Between Israel and a Future Palestinian State." *New York University Journal of International Law and Politics* 24, no. 4: 1399-1513.

Askhar, Ahmad. 1995. "Internal Refugees: Their Inalienable Right to Return." *News from Within*, 8 August, 14-17.

'Atiyyeh, Naser. 1993. "Patterns of Social Behavior among Marginal Groups in Palestinian Refugee Camps in Syria." *Jadal*, no. 4: 216-34.

Awartani, Hisham. 1994. "Palestinian-Israeli Economic Relations: Is Cooperation Possible?" In *The Economics of Middle East Peace*, edited by Stanley Fischer, Dani Rodrik, and Elias Tuma. Cambridge, MA: The MIT Press.

Ben-Ami, Shlomo. 1992. *Opening Remarks*. Official Presentation by the Israeli Delegation to the Refugee Working Group of the Middle East Peace Talks, 11 November, Ottawa, Canada. Mimeographed.

Ben Porath, Yoram, and Emanuel Marx. 1971. *Some Sociological and Economical Aspects of Refugee Camps on the West Bank*. Santa Monica, CA: The Rand Corporation.

Ben Porath, Yoram, Emanuel Marx, and Shimon Shamir. 1974. *A Refugee Camp on the Mountain Ridge*. Tel-Aviv: The Shiloah Center [Hebrew].

Benvenisti, Eyal, and Eyal Zamir. 1995. "Private Property Claims to Property Rights in the Future Israeli-Palestinian Settlement." *American Journal of International Law* 89, no. 2: 295-340.

Brand, Laurie A. 1988. *Palestinians in the Arab World*. New York: Columbia University Press.

____. 1995. "Palestinians and Jordanians: A Crisis of Identity." *Journal of Palestine Studies* 24, no. 4: 46-61.

Cahana, Shamay. 1993. *The Claim to a "Right of Return" for the Palestinians and Its Significance for Israel*. Jerusalem: Leonard David Institute, Hebrew University [Hebrew].

Cartin, Amnon. 1992. "Rehabilitation Plans for the Refugees in the Eastern Ghor in Jordan." *Research in the Geography of Israel* 13: 49-62 [Hebrew].

Cassese, Antonio. 1993. "Some Legal Observations on the Palestinian Right to Self-Determination." *The Oxford International Review* 4, no. 1: 10-13.

Cattan, Henry. 1969. *Palestine, the Arabs and Israel*. London: Longmans.

Center for Palestine Research and Studies (CPRS). 1995. *Results of Public Opinion Polls among Palestinians, 18-20 May 1995*. Nablus, West Bank: CPRS.

Cernea, Michael M. 1995. "Understanding and Preventing Impoverishment from Displacement: Reflections on the State of Knowledge." *Journal of Refugee Studies* 8, no. 3: 245-64.

Cervenak, C.M. 1984. "Promoting Inequality: Gender-Based Discrimination in UNRWA's Approach to Palestine Refugee Status." *Human Rights Quarterly* 16, no. 2: 300-74.

Chomsky, Noam. 1996. "A Painful Peace." *Z Magazine*, January, 37-50.

Efrat, Moshe. 1976. *The Palestinian Refugees: Economic and Social Research, 1949-1974.* Tel-Aviv: David Horowitz Institute, Tel-Aviv University [Hebrew].

_____. 1993. *The Palestinian Refugees: The Dynamics of Economic Integration in Their Host Countries.* Tel Aviv: Israeli International Institute for Applied Economic Policy Review.

Elmadmad, Khadija. 1993. "An Arab Declaration on the Protection of Refugees and Displaced Persons in the Arab World." *Journal of Refugee Studies* 6, no. 2: 173-75.

Elnajjar, Hassan. 1993. "Planned Emigration: The Palestinian Case." *International Migration Review* 27, no. 1: 34-50.

Endresen, Lena, and Elia Zureik. 1995. *Studies of Palestinian Refugees: A Bibliography.* Draft report, presented to the Refugee Working Group meeting held in Geneva, Swizerland, 12-15 December.

European Union. 1994. *Report Presented by the European Commission, Shepherd of the Social and Economic Infrastructure Theme, to the Refugee Working Group*, December.

Fischer, Stanley, Dani Rodrik, and Elias Tuma, eds. 1994. *The Economics of Middle East Peace.* Cambridge, MA: MIT Press.

Frelick, B. 1990. "The Right of Return." *International Journal of Refugee Law* 2, no. 3: 442-47.

Gazit, Shlomo. 1994a. "Fear of the Return," *Yediot Aharonot*, 18 May, p. 5 [Hebrew].

____. 1994b. *The Palestinian Refugee Problem*. Tel-Aviv: Jaffee Center for Strategic Studies, Tel-Aviv University [Hebrew].

Gilen, Signe, Are Hovdenak, Rania Maktabi, Jon Pedersen, and Dag Taustad. 1994. *Finding Ways: Palestinian Coping Strategies in Changing Environments*. Oslo: Norwegian Institute for Applied Social Science, FAFO Report 177.

Ginat, Joseph. 1994. *A Permanent Settlement Plan for the Palestinian Refugees*. Haifa: Haifa University (Available on the internet through gopher//gopher-igcc.ucsd.edu.).

Government of Israel. 1994. *The Refugee Issue: A Background Paper*. Jerusalem: Government Press Office.

____. 1996. *Guidelines of the Government of Israel* (Available on the internet through http://www.israel-mfa.gov.il.).

Hadawi, Sami, and Atef Kubursi. 1988. *Palestinian Rights and Losses in 1948: A Comprehensive Study*. London: Saqi Books.

Hagopian, Edward, and A.B. Zahlan. 1974. "Palestine's Arab Population: The Demography of Palestinians." *JPS* 3, 4: 32-73.

Hamed, Osama, and Radwan A. Sha'ban. 1994. "One-Sided Customs and Monetary Union: The Case of the West Bank and Gaza Strip under Israeli Occupation." In *The Economics of Middle East Peace*, edited by Stanley Fischer, Dani Rodrik, and Elias Tuma. Cambridge, MA: MIT Press.

Hanafi, Sari. 1995. "Les entrepreneurs en Syrie." In *L'Economie de la paix au Proche-Orient*, edited by L. Blin and Phillipe Fargues. Maisonneuve et Larose: CEDEJ.

Hannum, Hurst. 1987. *The Right to Leave and to Return in International Law and Practice*. Dodrecht, The Netherlands: Martinus Nijhoff Publishers.

Hathaway, James C. 1990. "A Reconsideration of the Underlying Premise of Refugee Law." *Harvard International Law Journal* 31: 129-83.

_____. 1991. *The Law of Refugee Status*. Toronto and Vancouver: Butterworths.

Hazboun, Samir. 1992. "A Socio-Economic Study of the Beit-Jibrin Refugee Camp, Bethlehem." *Journal of Arab Affairs* 2, no. 1: 54-67.

Heiberg, Marianne, Geir Ovensen, Heleg Brunborg, Rita Giacaman, Rema Hammami, Neil Hawkins, Hasan Abu Libdeh, Camilla Stoltenberg, Salim Tamari, Steinar Tamsfoss, Ole Fr. Ugland, and Lars Weiseth with special adviser Knud Knudsen. 1992. *Palestinian Society in Gaza, West Bank and Arab Jerusalem: A Survey of Living Conditions*, FAFO-Report 115, Oslo, Norway: Norwegian Institute for Applied Social Science.

Heller, Mark, and Sari Nusseibeh. 1991. *No Trumpets, No Drums: A Two-State Settlement of the Israeli-Palestinian Conflict*. New York: Hill and Wang.

Humphrey, M. 1993. "The Political Economy of Population Movements in the Middle East." *Middle East Report*, no. 181: 2-9.

Indyk, Martin. 1990. "The PLO Will Lose, Even if Iraq Wins." *New York Times*, 14 October.

International Labour Organization (ILO). 1994. Report of the Situation of Workers of the Occupied Territories, Appendix of Report of the Director General, 81st Session, Brussels: ILO.

Israeli-Palestinian Interim Agreement on the West Bank and Gaza Strip, Washington, 28 September 1995. 1996. In *Journal of Palestine Studies* 25, no. 2: 123-40.

Jaber, Abdel Tayseer. 1996. *The Situation of Palestinian Refugees in Jordan*. Amman, Jordan. January. Mimeographed.

Jerusalem Media and Communications Center (JMCC). 1994. *Israeli Obstacles to Economic Development in the Occupied Palestinian Territories*. Jerusalem: JMCC.

_____. 1995. *Poll: The Year of Autonomy*. Jerusalem: JMCC.

Kamal, Chafic. 1994. "Palestinians en Syrie. Visa pour l'avenir." *Les Cahiers de l'Orient*, no. 35: 113-20.

Kayali, Majid. 1996. "Palestinian Intellectuals in Syria Debate Current Palestinian Crisis: Causes, Problems and Questions." *Majallat al-Dirasat al-Filastiniyah*, no. 25: 123-54.

Khalidi, Rashid. 1989. "The Palestinian People: Twenty-Two Years After 1992." In *Intifada: The Palestinian Uprising Against Israeli Occupation*, edited by Zachary Lockman and Joel Beinin. Boston, MA: South End Press.

______. 1990. "Observations on the Palestinian Right of Return." In *The Palestinian Right of Return*. Cambridge, MA: The American Academy of Arts and Sciences, Paper no. 6.

______. 1994. "Toward a Solution." In *Palestinian Refugees: Their Problem and Future*. Washington, DC: The Center for Policy Analysis on Palestine.

Khalidi, Walid, ed. 1992. *All That Remains: The Palestinian Villages Occupied and Depopulated by Israel in 1948*. Washington, DC: Institute for Palestine Studies.

Khashan, Hilal. 1995. "Palestinian Resettlement in Lebanon: Behind the Debate." In *Palestinian Refugees: Background Papers*. Montreal, Quebec: Centre d'etudes arabes pour le development.

Kinsella, Kevin. 1991. *Palestinian Population Projections for 16 Countries of the World, 1990 to 2010*. Washington, DC: Bureau of the Census Center for International Research. Mimeographed.

Klinov, Ruth. 1995. *Reparations and Rehabilitation of Palestinian Refugees*. Jerusalem: Hebrew University. Mimeographed.

Kodmani-Darwish, Basma. 1994. *The Palestinian Question: A Fragmented Solution for a Dispersed People*. Ph.D. thesis, Institute d'Etudes Politique, Paris.

Kossaifi, George F. 1996. *The Palestinian Refugees' Right of Return.* Amman: The United Nations Economic and Social Commission for Western Asia.

Lapidoth, Ruth. 1986. "The Right of Return in International Law, with Special Reference to the Palestinian Refugees." *Israel Yearbook of Human Rights* 16: 103-25.

Lee, Luke T. 1993. "The Declaration of Principles of International Law and Compensation to Refugees: Its Significance and Implications." *Journal of Refugee Studies* 6, no. 1: 65-70.

Likud. *Likud Party Platform* (Available on the internet through http://www.israel-mfa.goc.il.).

Litani, Yehuda. 1988. "Arafat's Hesitant Step Forward." *Jerusalem Post (International Edition),* 26 November.

Mahmood, Sa'ld. 1990. *The Settling-In and Integrating Process of Internal Refugees in the Arab Sheltering Villages in the North of Israel, 1948-1986.* MA thesis, Department of Geography, Hebrew University, Jerusalem [Hebrew].

Marx, Emanuel. 1991. "Rehabilitation of Refugees in the Gaza Strip." *International Problems, Society and State* 5: 64-73 [Hebrew].

____. 1992. "Palestinian Refugee Camps in the West Bank and Gaza Strip." *Middle Eastern Studies* 28, no. 2: 281-94.

Masalha, Nur. 1992. *Expulsion of the Palestinians.* Washington, DC: Institute for Palestine Studies.

Maswada, Tayseer Abdel-Hafez. 1994. *The Demographic Characteristics of Palestinian Refugees in Syria, 1949-1992.* Ph.D. thesis, London University.

Memorandum Submitted by Palestinian Resistance Groups in Lebanon to the Prime Minister of Lebanon. 1994. Beirut, Lebanon.

Miller, Judith. 1991. *New York Times*, 16 June, E3.

Morris, Benny. 1987. *The Birth of the Palestinian Refugee Problem, 1947-1949*. Cambridge, UK: Cambridge University Press.

______. 1990. *1948 and After*. New York: Oxford University Press.

Mubanga-Chipoya, C.L.C. 1988. *Analysis of the Current Trends and Developments Regarding the Right to Leave Any Country Including One's Own, and to Return to One's Own Country, and Some Other Rights and Considerations Arising Therefrom*. Geneva: United Nations (Subcommission on Prevention of Discrimination and Protection of Minorities) (UN doc. E/C N.4/Sub./2/1988/35).

National Center for Educational Research and Development (NCERD). 1991. *The Socio-Economic Characteristics of Jordanian Returnees. Part 1, Statistical Analysis and Indicators*. Amman, Jordan: NCERD.

Natur, Suhail. 1993. *Conditions of the Palestinian People in Lebanon*. Beirut: Dar Al-Taqadum Al-Arabi.

Nir, Ori. 1995. "What is a Refugee? What is a Displaced Person?" *Ha'Aretz*, 7 March, B3.

Nour, Amer. 1993. *Coming Home: A Survey of the Socioeconomic Conditions of the West Bank and Gaza*. Jerusalem: Palestine Human Rights Information Center.

Palestine Liberation Organization (PLO). 1993. *Program for Development of the Palestinian National Economy for the Years 1994-2000*. Tunis: PLO.

Palestinian National Authority. 1995. *Palestinian Refugees and the Right of Return*. Jerusalem: Ministry of Information.

Pappé, Ilan. 1992. *The Making of the Arab-Israeli Conflict, 1947-51*. London: I.B. Tauris.

Peretz, Don. 1958. *Israel and the Palestine Arabs*. New York: AMS Press.

______. 1993. *Palestinians, Refugees and the Middle East Peace Process*. Washington, DC: United States Institute of Peace Press.

______. 1995. *Palestinian Refugee Compensation*. Washington, DC: The Center for Policy Analysis on Palestine.

Peron, Marc. 1995. *A Vision Paper of the New Middle East: A Perspective from the Refugee Working Group*. Ottawa.

"The Problem of Arab Refugees from Palestine." 1953. In Senate Committee on Foreign Relations, *U.S. Government Report of the Subcommittee on the Near East and Africa*, 24 July.

Quigley, John. 1992. "Family Reunion and the Right of Return to Occupied Territory." *Georgetown Immigration Law Journal* 6: 223-51.

Rabinovich, Itamar. 1990. "Israeli Perceptions of the Right to Return." In *The Palestinian Right of Return: Two Views*, edited by Jeffrey Boutwello. Cambridge, MA: The American Academy of Arts and Sciences, Paper no. 6.

Radi, Lamia. 1994. "Les Palestiniens du Koweit en Jordanie." *Monde Arabe Maghreb Mashrek*, no. 44 (avril-juin): 55-65.

Radley, Kurt Rene. 1978. "The Palestinian Refugees: The Right to Return in International Law." *American Journal of International Law* 72: 586-614.

Raei, Lamia Saleh. 1995. *The Forgotten Population: A Case Study of the Palestinians in Cairo*. M.A. thesis submitted to the Department of Anthropology, Sociology, and Psychology, American University in Cairo.

Reuters World Report. 1996. "Jordan Keeps Secret Palestinians' Population Rate." Report filed by Rana Sabagh, 27 January.

Richmond, Anthony H. 1994. *Global Apartheid. Refugees, Racism and the New World Order*. Toronto, New York, and Oxford: Oxford University Press.

Said, Edward, Ibrahim Abu-Lughod, Janet Abu-Lughod, Muhammad Hallaj, and Elia Zureik. 1990. *A Profile of the Palestinian People*. New York and Chicago: Palestine Human Rights Campaign.

Said, Edward. 1996. *Peace and Its Discontents,* with a preface by Christopher Hitchens. New York: Vintage Books.

Salam, Nawaf A. 1993. "Between Repatriation and Resettlement: Palestinian Refugees in Lebanon." *Journal of Palestine Studies* 24, no. 1: 18-27.

Savir, Uri. 1996. Address delivered on 5 May 1996 in Taba, Egypt at the opening of the final status talks (Available on the internet through http://www.israel-mfa.gov.il.).

Sayigh, Rosemary. 1995. "Palestinians in Lebanon: Harsh Present, Uncertain Future." *Journal of Palestine Studies* 25, no. 1: 37-53.

Schiff, Benjamin. 1989. "Between Occupier and Occupied: UNRWA and the West Bank and Gaza." *Journal of Palestine Studies* 18, no. 3: 60-75.

_____. 1991. "Assisting the Palestinian Refugees: Progress in Human Rights?" In *Progress in Postwar International Relations*, edited by Emanuel Heller and Beverly Crawford. New York: Columbia University Press.

_____. 1995. *Refugees Unto the Third Generation: UN Aid to Palestinians*. Syracuse, NY: Syracuse University Press.

Schiff, Ze'ev. 1996. "The Parties Met 20 Times in Europe and Israel." *Ha'Aretz,* 22 February.

Segal, Joel. 1996. *The West Bank and Gaza Strip: Phase Two* (Available on the internet through gopher://israel-info.gov.il.).

Sha'ban, Hussain. 1994. "What do the Palestinians Want in Lebanon?" *Majallat al-Dirasat al-Filastiniya*, no. 19: 176-77.

Sha'ban, Radwan and Samia A. Al-Botmeh. 1995. *Poverty in the West Bank, Gaza, and Jerusalem*. Jerusalem: Palestinian Economic Policy Research Institute.

Shami, Seteney. 1993. "The Social Implications of Population Displacement and Resettlement: An Overview with Focus on the Arab Middle East." *International Migration* 27: 4-32.

Shamir, Yitzhak. 1991. Address delivered on 31 October 1991 at the Madrid Conference (Available on the internet through http://www.israel-mfa.gov.il.).

Singer, Joel. 1995. *The West Bank and Gaza Strip: Phase Two* (Available on the internet through http://www.israel-mfa.gov.il.).

Statement of the Palestinian Side of the Joint Palestinian-Jordanian Delegation to the Middle East Peace Multilateral Conference. 13 May 1992, Ottawa, Canada.

Steinboim, Zvit. 1993. *The Palestinian Refugees: Portrait and Possible Solutions*. Tel-Aviv: Tel-Aviv University, The Armand Hammer Fund for Economic Cooperation in the Middle East [Hebrew].

Tadmor, Yoav. 1994. "The Palestinian Refugees of 1948: The Right to Compensation and Return." *Temple International Law Journal* 8, no. 2: 403-34.

Takkenberg, Lex. 1991. "The Protection of Palestinian Refugees in the Territories Occupied by Israel." *International Journal of Refugee Law* 3, no. 3: 414-34.

______. 1995. *Deprived of All Rights? The Status of Palestinian Refugees in International Law*. Ph.D. dissertation in progress, University of Nymegen, The Netherlands.

Tamari, Salim. 1994. *Critical Assessment of [the Bristol Report] Assistance to Refugees in the Middle East*. September. Mimeographed.

Tansley, Jill. 1996. *Adaptation in the West Bank and Gaza: A Discussion Paper*. Ottawa: International Development Research Center.

Tomeh, George, ed. 1975. *United Nations Resolutions on Palestine and the Arab-Israeli Conflict. Vol. 1: 1947-1974*. Washington, DC: Institute for Palestine Studies.

United Nations. 1952. *Annual Report of the Director General of UNRWA*, Doc.5224/5223, 25 November.

______. 1978. *The Right of Return of the Palestinian People*, published for the Committee on the Exercise of the Inalienable Rights of the Palestinian People. New York: United Nations.

______. 1979. *The Right of Self-Determination of the Palestinian People*, published by the Committee for the Exercise of the Inalienable Rights of the Palestinian People. New York: United Nations.

United Nations Conciliation Commission for Palestine: Report of the UN Economic Survey Mission for the Middle East. 1949. Doc. A/AC.25/6.

United Nations Development Program (UNDP). 1995. *At the Crossroads: Challenges and Choices for Palestinian Women in the West Bank and Gaza Strip*. New York: UNDP, Gender in Development Programs, United Nations.

United Nations Refugee and Works Agency (UNRWA). 1992a. *Family Reunification*. Vienna: UNRWA. October.

______. 1992b. *Social and Economic Infrastructure*. Vienna: UNRWA.

______. 1992c. *Socioeconomic Conditions in the Occupied Territory, Mid-1991/Mid-1992*. Vienna: UNRWA.

Viorst, Milton. 1989. *Reaching for the Olive Branch: UNRWA and Peace in the Middle East*. Washington, DC: Middle East Institute.

Watson, Andrew. 1994. *Economic Cooperation and Integration in the Middle East, with Particular Reference to Israel, Jordan, the West Bank and Gaza.* Toronto: Center for International Studies, University of Toronto.

Willigen, Van Loes. 1993. "Health Hazards of Organized Violence in Children: A View From Europe." *Journal of Refugee Studies* 6, no. 2: 176-82.

World Bank. 1993. *Developing the Occupied Territories: An Investment in Peace* (6 vols.). Washington, DC: World Bank.

World Organization of Jews from Arab Countries. 1994. *The Shape of the Arab-Israeli Settlement: Humanitarian and Demographic Issues. The Case of the Jews Who Left Arab Countries as Refugees.* Paper distributed at a seminar sponsored by the Council on Foreign Relations, 7 February, New York.

Zayyad, Ziad Abu. 1994. "The Palestinian Right of Return: A Realistic Approach." *Palestine-Israel Journal*, no. 2: 74-78.

Zedalis, Rex J. 1992. "Right to Return: A Close Look." *Georgetown Immigration Law Journal* 6: 495-517.

Zureik, Elia. 1995. "What State Palestine?" *Dissent*, 23-26.

_____. 1996. *The Trek Back Home: Palestinians Returning Home and the Problems of Adaptation.* Mimeographed.

Zureik, Elia, and Reza Nakhaie. 1995. *Educational Attainment in the West Bank, Gaza and East Jerusalem.* Mimeographed.

Zweig, Ronald W. 1993. "Restitution of Property and Refugee Rehabilitation: Two Case Studies." *Journal of Refugee Studies* 6, no. 1/4: 56-64.

Appendix 1: Map of Mandatory Palestine

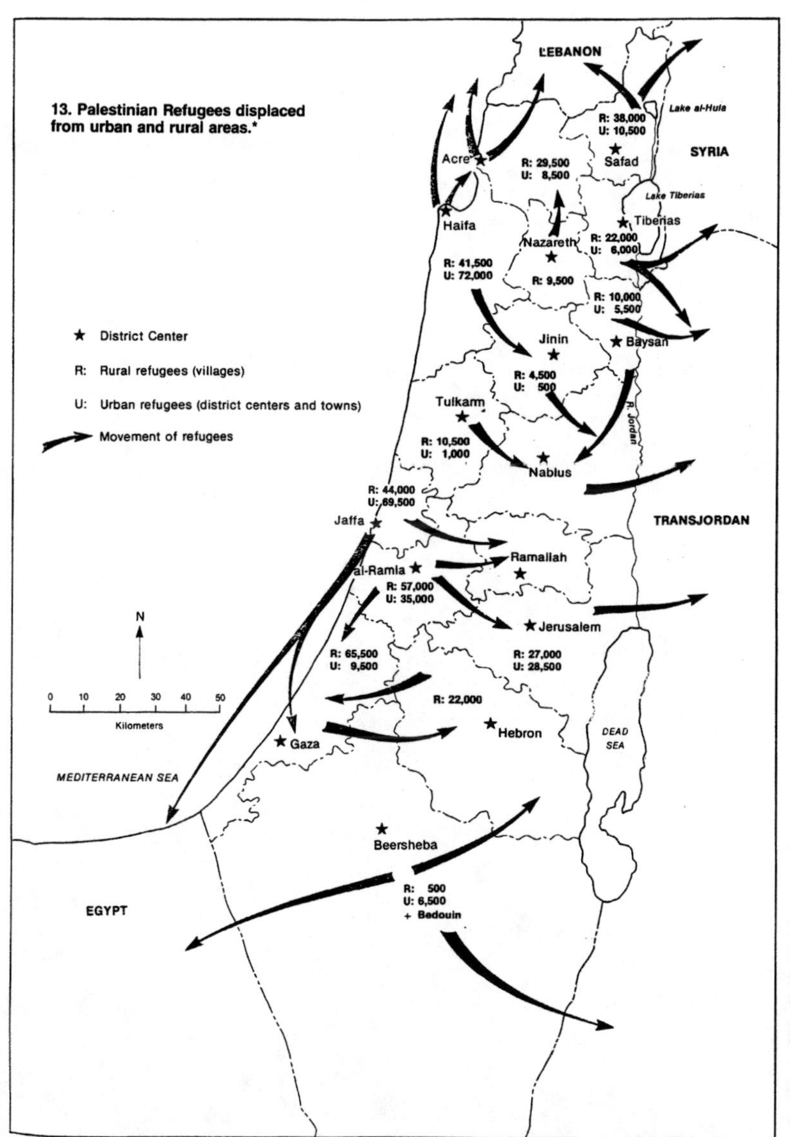

Source: Khalidi 1992.

Appendix 2: Resolution No. 194 (III) of 11 December 1948

Establishing a U.N. Conciliation Commission, resolving that Jerusalem should be placed under a permanent international regime, and resolving that the refugees should be permitted to return to their homes[1]

The General Assembly,
Having considered further the situation in Palestine,
1. *Expresses* its deep appreciation of the progress achieved through the good offices of the late United Nations Mediator in promoting a peaceful adjustment of the future situation of Palestine, for which cause he sacrificed his life; and
Extends its thanks to the Acting Mediator and his staff for their continued efforts and devotion to duty in Palestine;
2. *Establishes* a Conciliation Commission consisting of three States Members of the United Nations which shall have the following functions:
(a) To assume, in so far as it considers necessary in existing circumstances, the functions given to the United Nations Mediator on Palestine by resolution 186 (S-2) of the General Assembly of 14 May 1948;
(b) To carry out the specific function and directives given to it by the present resolution and such additional functions and directives as may be given to it by the General Assembly or by the Security Council;
(c) To undertake, upon the request of the Security Council, any of the functions now assigned to the United Nations Mediator on Palestine or to the United Nations Truce Commission by resolutions of the Security Council; upon such request to the Conciliation Commission by the Security Council with respect to all the remaining functions of the United Nations Mediator on Palestine under Security Council resolutions, the

---

[1]Text in Tomeh, pp. 15-17.

office of the Mediator shall be terminated;

3. *Decides* that a Committee of the Assembly, consisting of China, France, the Union of Soviet Socialist Republics, the United Kingdom and the United States of America, shall present, before the end of the first part of the present session of the General Assembly, for the approval of the Assembly, a proposal concerning the names of the three States which will constitute the Conciliation Commission;

4. *Requests* the Commission to begin its functions at once, with a view to the establishment of contact between the parties themselves and the Commission at the earliest possible date;

5. *Calls upon* the Governments and authorities concerned to extend the scope of negotiations provided for in the Security Council's resolution of 16 November 1948 and to seek agreement by negotiations conducted either with the Conciliation Commission or directly, with a view to the final settlement of all questions outstanding between them;

6. *Instructs* the Conciliation Commission to take steps to assist the Governments and authorities concerned to achieve a final settlement of all questions outstanding between them;

7. *Resolves* that the Holy Places--including Nazareth--religious buildings and sites in Palestine should be protected and free access to them assured, in accordance with existing rights and historical practice; that arrangements to this end should be under effective United Nations supervision; that the United Nations Conciliation Commission, in presenting to the fourth regular session of the General Assembly its detailed proposals for a permanent international regime for the territory of Jerusalem, should include recommendations concerning the Holy Places in that territory; that with regard to the Holy Places in the rest of Palestine the Commission should call upon the political authorities of the area concerned to give appropriate formal guarantees as to the protection of the Holy Places and access to them; and that these undertakings should be presented to the General Assembly for approval;

8. *Resolves* that, in view of its association with three world religions, the Jerusalem area, including the present municipality of Jerusalem *plus* the surrounding villages and towns, the most eastern of which shall be Abu Dis; the most southern, Bethlehem; the most western, Ein Karim (including also the built-up area of Mosta); and the most northern Shu'fat, should be accorded special and separate treatment from the rest of Palestine and should be placed under effective United Nations control;

Requests the Security Council to take further steps to ensure the demilitarization of Jerusalem at the earliest possible date;

Instructs the Commission to present to the fourth regular session of the General Assembly detailed proposals for a permanent international regime for the Jerusalem area which will provide for the maximum local autonomy for distinctive groups consistent with the special international status of the Jerusalem area;

The Conciliation Commission is authorized to appoint a United Nations representative, who shall co-operate with the local authorities with respect to the interim administration of the Jerusalem area;

9. *Resolves* that, pending agreement on more detailed arrangements among the Governments and authorities concerned, the freest possible access to Jerusalem by road, rail or air should be accorded to all inhabitants of Palestine;

Instructs the Conciliation Commission to report immediately to the Security Council, for appropriate action by that organ, any attempt by any party to impede such access;

10. *Instructs* the Conciliation Commission to seek arrangements among the Governments and authorities concerned which will facilitate the economic development of the area, including arrangements for access to ports and airfields and the use of transportation and communication facilities;

11. *Resolves* that the refugees wishing to return to their homes and live at peace with their neighbours should be permitted to do so at the earliest practicable date, and that compensation should be paid for the property of those choosing not to return and for loss of or damage to property which, under principles of international law or in equity, should be made good by the Governments or authorities responsible;

Instructs the Conciliation Commission to facilitate the repatriation, resettlement and economic and social rehabilitation of the refugees and the payment of their compensation, and to maintain close relations with the Director of the United Nations Relief for Palestine Refugees and, through him, with the appropriate organs and agencies of the United Nations;

12. *Authorizes* the Conciliation Commission to appoint such subsidiary bodies and to employ such technical experts, acting under its authority, as it may find necessary for the effective discharge of its functions and responsibilities under the present resolutions;

The Conciliation Commission will have its official headquarters at Jerusalem. The authorities responsible for maintaining order in Jerusalem will be responsible for taking all measures necessary to ensure the security of the Commission. The Secretary-General will provide a limited number of guards for the protection of the staff and premises of the Commission;

13. *Instructs* the Conciliation Commission to render progress reports periodically to the Secretary-General for transmission to the Security Council and to the Members of the United Nations.

14. *Calls upon* all Governments and authorities concerned to co-operate with the Conciliation Commission and to take all possible steps to assist in the implementation of the present resolution;

15. *Requests* the Secretary-General to provide the necessary staff and facilities and to make appropriate arrangements to provide the necessary funds required in carrying out the terms of the present resolution.

Appendix 3: Resolution No. 3236 (XXIX) of 22 November 1974

Recognizing The Rights of the Palestinian People[2]

The General Assembly,
Having considered the question of Palestine,
Having heard the statement of the Palestine Liberation Organization, the representative of the Palestinian people,
Having also heard other statements made during the debate,
Deeply concerned that no just solution to the problem of Palestine has yet been achieved and recognizing that the problem of Palestine continues to endanger international peace and security,
Recognizing that the Palestinian people is entitled to self-determination in accordance with the Charter of the United Nations,
Expressing its grave concern that the Palestinian people has been prevented from enjoying its inalienable rights, in particular its right to self-determination,
Guided by the purposes and principles of the Charter,
Recalling its relevant resolutions which affirm the right of the Palestinian people to self-determination,
1. *Reaffirms* the inalienable rights of the Palestinian people in Palestine, including:
(a) The right to self-determination without external interference;
(b) The right to national independence and sovereignty;
2. *Reaffirms also* the inalienable right of the Palestinians to return to their homes and property from which they have been displaced and uprooted, and calls for their return;

---

[2]Text in Tomeh, p. 111.

3. *Emphasizes* that full respect for and the realization of these inalienable rights of the Palestinian people are indispensable for the solution of the question of Palestine;

4. *Recognizes* that the Palestinian people is a principal party in the establishment of a just and durable peace in the Middle East;

5. *Further recognizes* the right of the Palestinian people to regain its rights by all means in accordance with the purposes and principles of the Charter of the United Nations;

6. *Appeals* to all States and international organizations to extend their support to the Palestinian people in its struggle to restore its rights, in accordance with the Charter;

7. *Requests* the Secretary-General to establish contacts with the Palestine Liberation Organization on all matters concerning the question of Palestine;

8. *Requests* the Secretary-General to report to the General Assembly at its thirtieth session on the implementation of the present resolution;

9. *Decides* to include the item entitled "Question of Palestine" in the provisional agenda of its thirtieth session.